SELECTED POEMS AND REFLECTIONS ON THE ART OF POETRY

SELECTED WORKS OF JULES SUPERVIELLE

Poetry
Gravitations (1925)
Le Forçat innocent (1930)
Les Amis inconnus (1934)
La Fable du monde (1938)
1939-1945. Poèmes (1946)
Oublieuse mémoire (1949)
Naissances (1951)
Le Corps tragique (1959)

Fiction
L'Homme de la Pampa (1923)
Le Voleur d'enfants (1926)
Le Survivant (1928)
L'Enfant de la haute-mer (1931)
L'Arche de Noé (1938)
Premiers Pas de l'Univers (1950)
Le Jeune Homme du Dimanche et des autres jours (1955)

Drama
La Belle au bois (1932)
Bolivar (1936)
Robinson (1949)
Shéhérazade (1949)
Le Voleur d'enfants (1949)
Les Suites d'une course (1959)

Selected Poems and Reflections on the Art of Poetry
by Jules Supervielle

Errata

Page	For	Read
13, 1. 22	souls	soul
23, 1. 21	anothing thing	another thing
93, 1. 13	was was	as was
111, 1. 5	the Betelgeuse	Betelgeuse
139, 1. 15	April	avril

SUN
347 W. 39th St., Apt. 7N
New York, N.Y. 10018

Selected Poems
and Reflections
on the Art of Poetry

Jules Supervielle

translated from the French
by George Bogin

NEW YORK

ACKNOWLEDGEMENTS

Some of these translations have appeared in *American Poetry Review, Chicago Review, New Letters, Ironwood,* and *Poetry East.*

Selections from DÉBARCADÈRES by Jules Supervielle copyright © 1966 by Editions Gallimard. Selections from GRAVITATIONS copyright © 1925 by Editions Gallimard. Selections from LE FORÇAT INNOCENT copyright © 1930 by Editions Gallimard. Selections from LES AMIS INCONNUS copyright © 1934 by Editions Gallimard. Selections from LA FABLE DU MONDE copyright © 1938 by Editions Gallimard. Selections from 1939-1945 (Poèmes) copyright © 1946 by Editions Gallimard. Selections from OUBLIEUSE MÉMOIRE copyright © 1949 by Editions Gallimard. Selections from NAISSANCES, including *En Songeant à un art poétique,* copyright © 1951 by Editions Gallimard. Selections from LE CORPS TRAGIQUE copyright © 1959 by Editions Gallimard.

Translation copyright © 1985 by George Bogin.

Printed in the United States of America

First Edition

Library of Congress Cataloging in Publication Data

Supervielle, Jules, 1884-1960.
  Selected poems and reflections on the art of poetry.

  1. Supervielle, Jules, 1884-1960 — Translations,
English. I. Title.
  PQ2637.U6A22   1984   841'.912   84-16392
  ISBN 0-915342-45-6 (Pbk.)

The publication of this book is supported by grants from the National Endowment for the Arts in Washington, D.C., a federal agency, and the New York State Council on the Arts.

176908

SELECTED POEMS AND REFLECTIONS ON THE ART OF POETRY

Contents

Preface   i

Débarcadères (1922)
Return to the Estancia [Retour à l'Estancia]   2

Gravitations (1925)
The Portrait [Le portrait]   8
47 Boulevard Lannes [47 Boulevard Lannes]   12
Prophecy [Prophétie]   18
Movement [Mouvement]   20
Without Walls [Sans murs]   22
Long Low Wave [Houle]   26
Fire! [Au feu!]   28

Le Forçat Innocent (1930)
Listen, Will You Learn to Hear Me from Afar [Ecoute,
   apprendras-tu à m'écouter de loin?   36
Oloron-Sainte-Marie [Oloron-Sainte-Marie]   38
Whisper in Agony [Whisper in Agony]   44
The Sun Speaks Softly [Le soleil parle bas]   46

Les Amis Inconnus (1934)
The Lane [L'allée]   50
The Stranger Among Us [Le hors-venu]   52
The Photographed Hands [Les mains photographiées]   56
Dawn in the Room [L'aube dans la chambre]   58
Longing for the Earth [Le regret de la terre]   60
Home Surrounded [La demeure entourée]   62
Shipwreck [Naufrage]   64
Visit of Night [Visite de la nuit]   66

La Fable du Monde (1938)
The Drop of Rain [La goutte de pluie]   70
Prayer to the Unknown [Prière à l'inconnu]   72
The Body [Le corps]   78

Beautiful Monster of the Night [Beau monstre de la nuit,
    palpitant de ténèbres]   80
The Child and the Stairs [L'enfant et les escaliers]   82
The Child and the River [L'enfant et la rivière]   84
It's You When You Have Left [C'est vous quand vous
    êtes partie]   86
Visages of Animals [Visages des animaux]   88
Docility [Docilité]   92
The Secret Sea [La mer secrète]   94
Horses without Riders [Chevaux sans cavaliers]   96

1939-1945 (1946)

1940 [1940]   100
Paris [Paris]   102
Night [La nuit . . .]   104
The Post House [Le relais]   106
Family of this World [Famille de ce monde]   108
Without Us [Sans nous]   112
Trees by Night and Day [Arbres dans la nuit et le jour]   116
If There Were No Trees at My Window [S'il n'était pas
    d'arbres à ma fenêtre]   120
To a Tree [A un arbre]   122
You Are Disappearing [Tu disparais]   124
The Dead Man Grieves [Le mort en peine]   126

Oublieuse Mémoire (1948)

BIRTH OF VENUS [NAISSANCE DE VENUS]   132
Champs-Elysées [Champs-Elysées]   136
The Sea [La mer]   140
First Days of the World [Premiers jours du monde]   144
War and Peace on Earth [Guerre et paix sur la terre]   146

Naissances (1951)
The Sick Man [Le malade]   152

Le Corps Tragique (1959)
Finale [Finale]   156

Reflections on the Art of Poetry (1951)   159

Reading Poetry in Public (1951)   169

Selected Poems
and Reflections
on the Art of Poetry

Preface

I, too, accept what many have said before me, that poetry in its full essence is untranslatable. I accept this and indeed profess it, but nevertheless find the challenge to translate irresistible. Obviously, I am not alone. Why, then, attempt the impossible? With me it is the desire to submerge myself in the poetry of another consciousness speaking in another language and to surface (perhaps triumphantly) with fresh, strange words from the deep—and a new poetry in my own language. I never cease feeling that the poem I have translated has become *my* poem. And in the transit from French into American English I find that I have been involved with yet another language, the universal unspoken mother tongue of which all spoken languages are only dialects.

Some poets are more amenable to translation than others and I believe that Supervielle is one of those. The image is central to his verse, as he himself says: "...most of the time I move forward in my thought only by means of images."[1] And what images! Cosmic, astonishing, unique! It is for them above all that I have wanted to translate Supervielle. If the translator is at least faithful to these images there is hope that the translated poem will have a communicable impact in any language, no matter how far removed from the French. When Supervielle writes as an orphan of his virtually never-known mother,

> "Ah, sur ta photographie
> Je ne puis pas même voir de quel côté souffle
>   ton regard...,"

and I say,

> "Ah, on your photograph
> I can't even see which way the wind of your glance
>   is blowing...,"[2]

I hope that my lines are being true to Supervielle, free in their American English and withal still under the spell of the French.

i

And when Supervielle also writes,

> "Boulevard Lannes que fais-tu si haut dans l'espace
> Et tes tombereaux que tirent des percherons l'un
>   derrière l'autre,
> Les naseaux dans l'éternité
> Et la queue balayant l'aurore?"

and I write,

> "Boulevard Lannes what are you doing up there in space
> With your tipcarts drawn by percherons one after
>   the other,
> Their nostrils in eternity
> And their tails sweeping the dawn?"[3]

I hope that these Superviellean images, too, can make their way into American poetry.

There is always the problem of communicating a poet's tone. Here, as well, Supervielle's simplicity and directness of address can only facilitate the task of the translator. Supervielle's persona is that of a supremely honest, kindly man who is comfortable in the cosmos and converses with the reader as with a friend. And he comforts the reader. This is rather unique in a time, the terrifying 20th century, when an appropriate malaise and fear grip most poets and their readers. Fear rarely enters the poetry of Supervielle, although he was a lifelong cardiac. The universals are there, to be sure, death especially, but with an equanimity that is truly surprising in a cosmopolitan who divided his life between Montevideo and Paris.[4] One would expect this from a pastoral poet, perhaps, but not an urban one. Still, he is not foolishly placid in the face of war or worse. Some of his most moving poems were written out of his grief over France's defeat and travail in World War II. And the last fifteen years of his life overlapped the first fifteen years of the atomic age. Long before, he had dared to envision the extinction of mankind, the end of the world, in his poem, "Prophecy,"[5] published in 1925:

> "Someday the earth will be
> Only a blind space turning. . ."

In 1959, the year before his death, he published in *Le Corps Tragique* the poem, "Finale,"[6] which again mythologizes the ultimate catastrophe.

Supervielle is an accessible poet, no small advantage for the translator. Though he takes risks up to the very edge of preciosity, he is never opaque. "Not writing for mystery specialists," he says, "I have always suffered when a sensitive person has not understood one of my poems."[7] In writing of the animals in Supervielle's poetry Claude Roy says, "He designs a squirrel or a rabbit with the minute precision of Dürer or Pisanello, then lets them loose in the décor of a canvas by Yves Tanguy."[8] Still, the surrealists cannot claim Supervielle although his poetry derives from dream and is often dream-like and phantasmagoric. There is no need for a key to the logic that regulates and illuminates his work. His poetry is nearly always open and transparent. He is a fabulist and mythmaker. A fresh wind blows through his poems, the wind of the pampa, the wind of the open ocean, gusting over Paris.

George Bogin

NOTES

1. "Reflections on the Art of Poetry," page 159.
2. "The Portrait," page 8.
3. "47 Boulevard Lannes," page 12.
4. Born Montevideo, 1884, died Paris, 1960.
5. Page 18.
6. Page 156.
7. "Reflections on the Art of Poetry."
8. *Jules Supervielle*, Seghers, Paris, 1970. Tanguy, French surrealist painter, 1900-1955.

iii

Débarcadères
1922

Le petit trot des gauchos me façonne,
Les oreilles fixes de mon cheval m'aident à me situer.
Je retrouve dans sa plénitude ce que je n'osais plus envisager,
même par une petite lucarne,
toute la pampa étendue à mes pieds comme il y a sept ans.
O mort! me voici revenu.
J'avais pourtant compris que tu ne me laisserais pas revoir ces
terres,
une voix me l'avait dit qui ressemblait à la tienne et tu ne
ressembles qu'à toi-même.
Et aujourd'hui, je suis comme ce hennissement qui ne sait pas
que tu existes,
je trouve étrange d'avoir tant douté de moi et c'est de toi
que je doute ô Surfaite,
même quand mon cheval enjambe les os d'un boeuf proprement
blanchis par les vautours et par les aigles,
ou qu'une odeur de bête fraîchement écorchée, me tord le nez
quand je passe.
Je fais corps avec la pampa qui ne connaît pas la mythologie,
avec le désert orgueilleux d'être le désert depuis les temps
les plus abstraits,
il ignore les Dieux de l'Olympe qui rythment encore le vieux
monde.
Je m'enfonce dans la plaine qui n'a pas d'histoire et tend de
tous côtés sa peau dure de vache qui a toujours couché
dehors
et n'a pour toute végétation que quelques talas, ceibos, pitas,
qui ne connaissent le grec ni le latin,
mais savent résister au vent affamé du pôle,
de toute leur ruse barbare
en lui opposant la croupe concentrée de leur branchage
grouillant d'épines et leurs feuilles en coup de hache.
Je me mêle à une terre qui ne rend de comptes à personne et
se défend de ressembler à ces paysages manufacturés
d'Europe, saignés par les souvenirs,

Return to the Estancia

The jog trot of the gauchos shapes me,
the pricked up ears of my horse help me to place myself.
I find again in its plenitude what I no longer dared to envisage,
even through a little garret window—
all the pampa spread out at my feet as though it was seven
    years ago.
Oh Death, here I am back again!
It was my understanding, though, that you would not let me
    see these lands again.
A voice resembling yours told me so and you resemble only
    yourself
and today I am like this neighing which does not know you
    exist.
I find it strange to have doubted myself so much and it is you
    whom I really doubt, Oh Overrated One,
even when my horse leaps over the bones of a steer cleanly
    whitened by the vultures and the eagles
or when the odor of a freshly skinned animal puckers my nose
    when I pass.
I am one with the pampa which knows nothing of mythology,
with the desert proud of being the desert from the most abstract
    times—
it is unaware of the Gods of Olympus who still rhythm the old
    world.
I bury myself in the plain which has no history and spreads out
    on all sides its tough cowhide which has always slept
    outdoors
and has for vegetation only some talas, ceibos and pitas
which don't know Greek or Latin
but know how to resist the ravenous wind of the Pole
with all their barbaric guile
by opposing it with the massed rumps of their branches
    swarming with thorns and with crude leaves.
I mingle with a land which accounts to no one and defends
    itself from resembling those landscapes manufactured in
    Europe, bloodied by memories,

à cette nature extenuée et poussive qui n'a plus que des quintes
de lumière,
et, repentante, efface, l'hiver, ce qu'elle fit pendant l'été.

J'avance sous un soleil qui ne craint pas les intempéries,
et se sert sans lésiner de ses pots de couleur locale toute
fraîche
pour des ciels de plein vent qui vont d'une fusée jusqu'au zénith,
et il saisit dans ses rayons, comme au lasso, un gaucho monté,
tout vif.

Les nuages ne sont pas pour lui des prétextes à une mélancolie
distinguée,
mais de rudes amis d'une autre race, ayant d'autres habitudes,
avec lesquels on peut causer,
et les orages courts sont de brusques fêtes communes
où ciel, soleil et nuages
y vont de bon coeur et tirent jouissance de leur propre plaisir
et de celui des autres,
où la pampa
roule ivre-morte dans la boue palpitante où chavirent les
lointains,
jusqu'à l'heure des hirondelles
et des derniers nuages, le dos rond dans le vent du sud,
quand la terre, sur tout le pourtour de l'horizon bien accroché,
sèche ses flaques, son bétail et ses oiseaux
au ciel retentissant des jurons du soleil qui cherche à rassembler
ses rayons dispersés

Janvier 1920

4

with this exhausted and shortwinded nature which possesses
      wisdom only in fits
and, repentant, expunges in the winter what it made in the
      summer.
I move on under a sun which has no fear of bad weather
and serves up without stint fresh pots of local color
for skies with great winds that rocket up to the zenith—
and seizes in its rays, like a lasso, a mounted gaucho utterly
      alive.
The clouds are not at all for him pretexts for a distinguished
      melancholy,
but impetuous friends of another race, having other customs,
      with whom one can converse
and the brief tempests are like sudden communal feasts
where sky, sun and clouds
attend good-naturedly and enjoy their own pleasure and that of
      others,
where the pampa
rolls dead-drunk in the palpitating mud and the distances
      capsize
up to the very hour of the swallows and the last clouds,
where the earth, along the entire periphery of the suspended
      horizon,
dries its puddles, its cattle and its birds
under a heaven resounding with the oaths of the sun which is
      seeking to assemble its scattered rays.

January 1920

Gravitations
1925

Le portrait

Mère, je sais très mal comme l'on cherche les morts,
Je m'égare dans mon âme, ses visages escarpés,
Ses ronces et ses regards.
Aide-moi à revenir
De mes horizons qu'aspirent des lèvres vertigineuses,
Aide-moi à être immobile,
Tant des gestes nous séparent, tant de lévriers cruels!
Que je penche sur la source où se forme ton silence
Dans un reflet de feuillage que ton âme fait trembler.
Ah! sur ta photographie
Je ne puis pas même voir de quel côté souffle ton regard.
Nous nous en allons pourtant, ton portrait avec moi-même,
Si condamnés l'un à l'autre
Que notre pas est semblable
Dans ce pays clandestin
Où nul ne passe que nous.
Nous montons bizarrement les côtes et les montagnes
Et jouons dans les descentes comme des blessés sans mains.
Un cierge coule chaque nuit, gicle à la face de l'aurore,
L'aurore qui tous les jours sort des draps lourds de la mort,
A demi asphyxiée,
Tardant à se reconnaître.

Je te parle durement, ma mère,
Je parle durement aux morts parce qu'il faut leur parler dur,
Pour dominer le silence assourdissant
Qui voudrait nous séparer, nous les morts et les vivants.
J'ai de toi quelques bijoux comme des fragments de l'hiver
Qui descendent les rivières.
Ce bracelet fut de toi qui brille en la nuit d'un coffre
En cette nuit écrasée où le croissant de la lune
Tente en vain de se lever
Et recommence toujours, prisonnier de l'impossible.

The Portrait

Mother, I'm not very good at looking for the dead,
I'm going astray in my soul with its steep faces,
Its brambles and its stares.
Help me to come back
From my horizons breathed in from dizzying lips.
Help me to be motionless,
So many gestures separate us, so many cruel greyhounds!
Let me lean over the spring where your silence forms
In a reflection of foliage set trembling by your soul.
Ah, on your photograph
I can't even see which way the wind of your glance is blowing.
We go off, nevertheless, your portrait with myself,
So condemned to each other
That our step is similar
In this clandestine country
Where no one goes but us.
Strangely we climb the hills and the mountains
And act in the descents like wounded without hands.
A church candle gutters each night, spurts out in the face
      of the dawn,
The dawn which emerges every day from the heavy sheets
      of death,
Half-suffocated,
A long time coming to itself.

I speak harshly to you, my mother,
I speak harshly to the dead because it is necessary to talk hard
      to them
In order to dominate the deafening silence
That would separate us, the dead from the living.
I have a few jewels you left me like fragments of winter
That flow down the rivers.
This bracelet of yours gleams in the night of a chest of drawers
In the crushed night where the crescent of the moon
Tries hopelessly to lift itself
And always begins again, prisoner of the impossible.

9

J'ai été toi si fortement, moi qui le suis si faiblement,
Et si rivés tous les deux que nous eussions dû mourir ensemble,
Comme deux matelots mi-noyés, s'empêchant l'un l'autre de nager,
Se donnant des coups de pied dans les profondeurs de l'Atlantique
Où commencent les poissons aveugles
Et les horizons verticaux.

Parce que tu as été moi
Je puis regarder un jardin sans penser à autre chose,
Choisir parmi mes regards,
M'en aller à ma rencontre.
Peut-être reste-t-il encore
Un ongle de tes mains parmi les ongles de mes mains,
Un de tes cils mêlé aux miens;
Un de tes battements s'égare-t-il parmi les battements de mon
    coeur,
Je le reconnais entre tous
Et je sais le retenir.

Mais ton coeur bat-il encore? Tu n'as plus besoin de coeur,
Tu vis séparée de toi comme si tu étais ta propre soeur,
Ma morte de vingt-huit ans,
Me regardant de trois-quarts,
Avec l'âme en équilibre et pleine de retenue.
Tu portes la même robe que rien n'usera plus,
Elle est entrée dans l'éternité avec beaucoup de douceur
Et change parfois de couleur, mais je suis seul à savoir.

Anges de marbre, lions de bronze, et fleurs de pierre,
C'est ici que rien ne respire.
Et voici à mon poignet
Les pouls minéral des morts,
Celui-là que l'on entend si l'on approche le corps
Des strates du cimetière.

I have been you so strongly, I who am now so feebly you,
And so riveted together that we ought to have died together,
Like two half-drowned sailors impeding each other
    from swimming,
Kicking each other in the depths of the Atlantic
Where the blind fish start
And the vertical horizons.

Because you have been me
I can look at a garden without thinking of something else,
Can choose among my expressions,
Can go off to encounter myself.

Perhaps there still lives on
A nail from your hands among the nails of my hands,
One of your eyelashes mingled with mine,
One of your throbbings astray among the throbbings of
    my heart.
I recognize it among them all
And know how to safeguard it.

But does your heart still beat? You don't need heart anymore.
You live separated from yourself as though you were your
    own sister,
My dead one of twenty-eight
Looking at me from a three-quarter portrait
With your soul in equilibrium and full of reticence.
You wear the same dress that nothing will wear out anymore.
It has entered eternity with much sweetness
And changes color sometimes, but I'm the only one to know.

Angels of marble, lions of bronze, and flowers of stone,
Here nothing breathes
And here in my wrist,
Beats the mineral pulse of the dead,
The pulse that one hears when one's body approaches
The layers of the cemetery.

47 Boulevard Lannes

à Marcel Jouhandeau

Boulevard Lannes, que fais-tu si haut dans l'espace
Et tes tombereaux que tirent des percherons l'un derrière
    l'autre,
Les naseaux dans l'éternité
Et la queue balayant l'aurore?
Le charretier suit, le fouet levé,
Une bouteille dans sa poche.
Chaque chose a l'air terrestre et vit dans son naturel.
Boulevard Lannes, que fais-tu au milieu du ciel
Avec tes immeubles de pierre que viennent flairer les années,
Si à l'écart du soleil de Paris et de sa lune
Que le réverbère ne sait plus s'il faut qu'il s'éteigne ou s'allume,
Et que la laitière se demande si ce sont bien des maisons,
Avançant de vrais balcons,
Et si tintent à ses doigts des flacons de lait ou des mondes?
Près du ruisseau, un balayeur de feuilles mortes de platanes
En forme un tas pour la fosse commune de tous les platanes
Echelonnées dans le ciel.
Ses mouvements font un bruit aéré d'immensité
Que l'âme voudrait imiter.
Ce chien qui traverse la chaussée miraculeusement
Est-ce encore un chien respirant?
Son poil sent la foudre et la nue
Mais ses yeux restent ingénus
Dans la dérivante atmosphère
Et je doute si le boulevard
N'est pas plus large que l'espace entre le Cygne et Bételgeuse.
Ah! si je colle l'oreille à l'immobile chaussée
C'est l'horrible galop des mondes, la bataille des vertiges;
Par la fente des pavés
Je vois que s'accroche une étoile
A sa propre violence
Dans l'air creux insaisissable
Qui s'enfuit de toutes parts.

47 Boulevard Lannes

to Marcel Jouhandeau

Boulevard Lannes, what are your doing up there in space
With your tipcarts drawn by percherons one after the other,
Their nostrils in eternity
And their tails sweeping the dawn?
The driver follows, his whip up,
A bottle in his pocket.
Each thing has an earthly appearance and lives in its
    own nature.
Boulevard Lannes, what are you doing in the middle of the sky
With your apartment houses of stone that the years come
    to sniff,
So remote from the sun of Paris and its moon
That the street lamp no longer knows whether to extinguish
    itself or to light up
And the milkmaid asks herself if those are really houses
Moving forward with real balconies,
And if those are milkbottles tinkling in her fingers, or worlds?
Near the brook a sweeper of dead plane tree leaves
Makes a heap for the common ditch of all the plane trees
Spread out in the sky.
His movements make a noise aerated with immensity
Which the souls would like to imitate.
This dog who crosses the road miraculously—
Is he still a breathing dog?
His fur feels the lightning and the cloud
But his eyes remain ingenuous
In the drifting atmosphere.
And I doubt if the boulevard
Is wider than the space between Cygnus and Betelgeuse.
Ah, if I press my ear against the motionless road
I hear the horrible gallop of worlds, the battle of vertigoes;
Through a crack in the pavement
I see that a star is caught
In its own violence
In the unseizable, unsubstantial air
That slips away on all sides.

Caché derrière un peu de nuit comme par une colonne,
En étouffant ma mémoire qui pourrait faire du bruit,
Je guette avec mes yeux d'homme
Mes yeux venus jusqu'ici,
Par quel visage travestis?
Autour de moi je vois bien que c'est l'année ou nous sommes
Et cependant on dirait le premier jour du monde,
Tant les choses se regardent fixement,
Entourées d'un mutisme différent.

Ce pas lourd sur le trottoir
Je le reconnais, c'est le mien,
Je l'entends partir au loin,
Il s'est séparé de moi
(Ne lui suis-je donc plus rien)
S'en va maintenant tout seul,
Et se perd au fond du Bois.
Si je crie on n'entend rien
Que la plainte de la Terre,
Palpant vaguement sa sphère,
A des millions de lieues,
S'assurant de ses montagnes,
De ses fleuves, ses forêts,
Attisant sa flamme obscure
Où se chauffe le futur
(Il attend que son tour vienne.)

Je reste seul avec mes os
Dont j'entends les blancheurs confuses:
"Où va-t-il entre deux ciels, si froissé par ses pensées,
Si loin de la terre ferme
Le voilà qui cherche l'ombre et qui trouve du soleil."

Puisque je reconnais la face de ma demeure dans cette altitude,
Je vais accrocher les portraits de mon père et de ma mère
Entre deux étoiles tremblantes;
Je poserai la pendule ancienne du salon
Sur une cheminée taillée dans la nuit dure,

Hidden behind a bit of night as by a column,
Hushing my memory which is liable to be noisy,
I'm on the lookout with my human eyes,
My eyes that have come precisely here,
Through what masked face?
Around me I see clearly that it's this year—
However, it seems to be the first day of the world,
So many things stare at themselves fixedly
Surrounded by such varied speechlessness.

This heavy step on the sidewalk—
I recognize it, it's mine,
I hear it leave in the distance,
It's separated from me
(Am I nothing to it anymore?)
It goes off all alone now
And loses itself in the depths of the Bois.
If I cry out no one hears anything
But the moan of the Earth
Vaguely fingering her sphere
Of a million leagues,
Assuring herself of her mountains,
Her rivers, her forests,
Fanning the dark flame
Where the future warms itself
(It's waiting for its turn to come.)

I stand alone with my bones
Hearing their confused whitenesses:
"Where is he going, between two skies, so crumpled by
    his thoughts,
So far from terra firma—
Look at him seeking the shade and finding the sun."

Since I recognize the face of my house up here
I'm going to hang the portraits of my father and my mother
Between two trembling stars.
I'll stand the ancient clock from the living room
On a carved mantelpiece in the hard night

Et le savant qui un jour les découvrira dans le ciel
En chuchotera jusqu'à sa mort.
Mais il faudra très longtemps pour que sa main aille et vienne
Comme si elle manquait d'air, de lumière et d'amis,
Dans le ciel endolori
Qui faiblement se plaindra
Sous les angles des objets qui seront montés de la Terre.

And the scholar who will discover them in the sky someday
Will whisper over them up to the moment of his death.
But it will have to be a very long time for my hand
    to come and go
As if it were lacking air, light and friends
In the aching sky
Which will feebly moan to itself
Under the angles of the objects which will have mounted from
    the Earth.

Prophétie
à Jean Cassou.

Un jour la Terre ne sera
Qu'un aveugle espace qui tourne,
Confondant la nuit et le jour.
Sous le ciel immense des Andes
Elle n'aura plus de montagnes,
Même pas un petit ravin.

De toutes les maisons du monde
Ne durera plus qu'un balcon
Et de l'humaine mappemonde
Une tristesse sans plafond.
De feu l'Océan Atlantique
Un petit goût salé dans l'air,
Un poisson volant et magique
Qui ne saura rien de la mer.

D'un coupé de mil-neuf-cent-cinq
(Les quatre roues et nul chemin!)
Trois jeunes filles de l'époque
Restées à l'état de vapeur
Regarderont par la portière
Pensant que Paris n'est pas loin
Et ne sentiront que l'odeur
Du ciel qui vous prend à la gorge.

A la place de la forêt
Un chant d'oiseau s'élèvera
Que nul ne pourra situer,
Ni préférer, ni même entendre,
Sauf Dieu qui, lui, l'écoutera
Disant: "C'est un chardonneret."

Prophecy
to Jean Cassou

Someday the Earth will be
Only a blind space turning,
Confounding night with day.
Under the vast sky of the Andes
There will be no more mountains,
Not even a small ravine.

Of all the houses in the world
Only a balcony will endure
And of the human map of the world
Sorrow without a ceiling.
Of the late Atlantic Ocean
A little salty taste in the air
And a fish flying and magical
That will know nothing of the sea.

Of a 1905 coupe
(four wheels and no road!)
Three young girls of the time
Persisting in a state of mist
Will peer out of the door
Thinking that Paris isn't far
And will smell only the odor
Of sky which grips you by the throat.

Where the forest was
A birdsong will arise
Which no one will ever be able to place
Or prefer or even hear
But God Himself, who, listening,
Will say, "That's a goldfinch."

Mouvement

Ce cheval qui tourna la tête
Vit ce que nul n'a jamais vu
Puis il continua de paître
A l'ombre des eucalyptus.

Ce n'était ni homme ni arbre
Ce n'était pas une jument
Ni même un souvenir de vent
Qui s'exerçait sur du feuillage.

C'était ce qu'un autre cheval,
Vingt mille siècles avant lui,
Ayant soudain tourné la tête
Aperçut à cette heure-ci.

Et ce que nul ne reverra,
Homme, cheval, poisson, insecte,
Jusqu'à ce que le sol ne soit
Que le reste d'une statue
Sans bras, sans jambes et sans tête.

Movement

This horse who turned his head
Saw what no one has ever seen,
Then continued to graze
In the shadow of the eucalyptus.

It was neither man nor tree,
It wasn't a mare
Nor even a memory of wind
Exercising itself in the foliage.

It was what another horse
Twenty thousand centuries before him,
Suddenly turning its head,
Glimpsed at this very hour.

And that which no creature will see again,
Man, horse, fish, insect,
Until the soil itself becomes
No more than the remains of a statue
Without arms, legs or head.

Sans Murs

à Ramón Gómez de la Serna.

Tout le ciel est taché d'encre comme les doigts d'un enfant.
Où l'école et le cartable?
Dissimule cette main—elle aussi a des taches noires—
Sous le bois de cette table.
Quarante visages d'enfants divisent ma solitude.
Qu'ai-je fait de l'océan,
Dans quel aérien désert sont morts les poissons volants?
J'ai seize ans par le monde et sur les hautes montagnes,
J'ai seize ans sur les rivières et autour de Notre Dame,
Dans la classe de Janson
Où je vois le temps passer sur le cadran de mes paumes.
Le bruit de mon coeur m'empêche d'écouter le professeur.
J'ai déjà peur de la vie avec ses souliers ferrés
Et ma peur me fait si honte que j'égare mon regard
Dans un lointain où ne peut comparaître le remords.
Le pas des chevaux sur l'asphalte brille dans mon âme humide
Et se reflète à l'envers, entrecroisé de rayons.
Une mouche disparaît dans les sables du plafond.
Le latin autour de nous campe et nous montre sa lèpre;
Je n'ose plus rien toucher sur la table de bois noir.
Lorsque je lève les yeux, à l'Orient de la chaire
Je vois une jeune fille, de face comme la beauté,
De face comme la douleur, comme la nécessité.
Une jeune fille est assise, elle fait miroiter son coeur
Comme un bijou plein de fièvre aux distantes pierreries.
Un nuage de garçons glisse toujours vers ses lèvres
Sans qu'il paraisse avancer.
On lui voit une jarretière, elle vit loin des plaisirs,
Et la jambe demi-nue, inquiète, se balance.
La gorge est si seule au monde que nous tremblons qu'elle
     ait froid,
(Est-ce ma voix qui demande si l'on peut fermer les fenêtres?)
Elle aimerait à aimer tous les garçons de la classe,

Without Walls

to Ramón Gómez de la Serna

The whole sky is stained with ink like the fingers of a child.
Where is the school and the schoolbag?
Hide this hand—it, too, has black stains—
Under the wood of this table.
The faces of forty children share my solitude.
What have I done with the ocean,
In what aerial desert did the flying fish die?
I'm sixteen all over the world and on the high mountains,
I'm sixteen on the rivers and around Notre Dame
And in the classroom at Janson-de-Sailly
Where I see time pass on the dial of my palms.
The noise of my heart prevents me from listening
        to the teacher.
I'm already afraid of life with its hobnailed shoes
And my fear makes me so ashamed that my glance wanders
Into a distance where remorse can't appear.
The walk of the horses on the asphalt shines in my damp soul
And is reflected upside down intertwined with rays.
A fly disappears in the sands of the ceiling,
The Latin around us squats and shows us its leprosy—
I don't dare touch anothing thing on the black wooden table.
When I lift my eyes to the Orient of the teacher's desk
I see a young girl facing us like beauty itself,
Facing us like pain, like necessity.
A young girl sits there, she makes her heart sparkle
Like a jewel full of fever to distant precious stones.
A cloud of boys is gliding toward her lips
Without ever seeming to get closer.
We glimpse her garter, she lives far from pleasures
And her half-naked leg, uneasy, swings back and forth.
Her bosom is so alone in the world that we tremble that she
        might be cold,
(Is it my voice which is asking if the windows can be shut?)
She would love to love all the boys in the class,

La jeune fille apparue,
Mais sachant qu'elle mourra si le maître la découvre
Elle nous supplie d'être obscurs afin de vivre un moment
Et d'être une jolie fille au milieu d'adolescents.
La mer dans un coin du globe compte, recompte ses vagues
Et prétend en avoir plus qu'il n'est d'étoiles au ciel.

This young girl who has appeared among us
But knowing that she'll die if the teacher discovers her
She begs us to be discreet so she can live for a moment
And be a pretty girl in the midst of adolescents.
The sea in a corner of the globe counts and recounts its waves
And pretends to have more of them than there are stars
    in the sky.

Houle

Vous auberges et routes, vous ciels en jachère,
Vous campagnes captives des mois de l'année,
Forêts angoissées qu'étouffe la mousse,
Vous m'éveillez la nuit pour m'interroger.
Voici un peuplier qui me touche du doigt,
Voici une cascade qui me chante à l'oreille,
Un affluent fiévreux s'élance dans mons coeur,
Une étoile soulève, abaisse mes paupières
Sachant me déceler parmi morts et vivants
Même si je me cache dans un herbeux sommeil
Sous le toit voyageur du rêve.
Depuis les soirs apeurés que traversait le bison
Jusqu'à ce matin de mai qui cherche encore sa joie
Et dans mes yeux mensongers n'est peut-être qu'une fable,
La terre est une quenouille que filent lune et soleil
Et je suis un paysage échappé de ses fuseaux,
Une vague de la mer naviguant depuis Homère
Recherchant un beau rivage pour que bruissent trois mille ans.

La mémoire humaine roule sur le globe, l'enveloppe,
Lui faisant un ciel sensible innervé à l'infini,
Mais les bruits gisent fauchés dans les siècles révolus
L'histoire n'a pas encor pu faire entendre une voix.
Et voici seul sur la route planétaire notre coeur
Flambant comme du bois sec entre deux monts de silence
Qui sur lui s'écrouleront au vent mince de la mort.

Long Low Wave

You inns and roads, you fallow-lying skies,
You countrysides, captives of the months of the year,
Anguished forests that smother your moss,
You wake me at night to question me.
Here is a poplar that touches me with its finger,
Here a cascade that sings in my ear,
A feverish tributary surges into my heart,
A star raises and lowers my eyelids,
Knowing how to detect me among the dead and the living
Even if I hide myself in a grassy sleep
Under the wayfaring roof of dream.
Ever since the frightened evenings that the bison crossed
As far as this May morning still looking for its joy
And in my lying eyes is only a myth, perhaps,
The earth has been a distaff spun by the moon and sun
And I am a landscape slipped off her spindles,
A wave of the sea sailing since Homer
Seeking again the beautiful shore that three thousand years
        murmur for.

Human memory rolls around the globe, envelops it,
Creating a sensitive sky that supplies nerves to the infinite,
But its sounds lie buried, crushed flat in the bygone centuries
And History has still not been able to make its voice heard.
And here alone on the planetary road is our heart
Flaming like dry wood between two hills of silence
Which will collapse on it in the thin wind of death.

Au feu!

à Henri Michaux.

J'enfonce les bras levés vers le centre de la Terre
Mais je respire, j'ai toujours un sac de ciel sur la tête
Même au fort des souterrains
Qui ne savent rien du jour.
Je m'écorche à des couches d'ossements
Qui voudraient me tatouer les jambes pour me reconnaître
      un jour.
J'insulte un squelette d'iguanodon, en travers de mon passage,
Mes paroles font grenaille sur la canaille de ses os,
Et je cherche à lui tirer ses oreilles introuvables
Pour qu'il ne me barre plus la route,
Mille siècles après sa mort,
Avec le vaisseau de son squelette qui fait nuit de toutes parts.
Ma colère prend sur moi une avance circulaire,
Elle déblaie le terrain, canonne les profondeurs.
Je hume des formes humaines à de petites distances
Courtes, courtes.
J'y suis.
Voici les hautes statues de marbre qui lèvent l'index avant
      de mourir.
Un grand vent gauche, essouflé, tourne sans trouver une issue.
Que fait-il au fond de la Terre? Est-ce le vent des suicidés?
Quel est mon chemin parmi ces milliers de chemins qui
      se disputent à mes pieds
Un honneur que je devine?
Peut-on demander sa route à des hommes considerés
      comme morts
Et parlant avec un accent qui ressemble à celui du silence.
Centre de la Terre! je suis un homme vivant.
Ces empereurs, ces rois, ces premiers ministres, entendez-les
      qui me font leurs offres de service,
Parce que je trafique à la surface avec les étoiles et la
      lumière du jour.
J'ai le beau rôle avec les morts, les mortes et les mortillons.
Je leur dis: "Voyez-moi ce coeur,

Fire!

to Henri Michaux

I thrust my arms toward the center of the Earth
And breathe—I always carry a sackful of sky on my head
Even in the depths of the subterranean passages
Which know nothing of day.
I scrape myself against the layers of bones
Which would like to tattoo my legs to identify me someday.
I insult the skeleton of an iguanodon lying across my path.
My words are buckshot against the rabble of its bones
And I look to pull its undiscoverable ears
So that it can't go on barring the way
A thousand centuries after its death
With the vessel of its skeleton leaking night everywhere.
My anger circles ahead of me
And sweeps the terrain, bombards the depths.
I take in human shapes a little way off—
Closer, closer.
I am there.
There are high marble statues here that raise their index
        fingers before dying.
A big clumsy wind, out of breath, wheels without finding
        a way out.
What is it doing at the bottom of the Earth? Is it the wind
        of the suicides?
What is my path among the thousands of paths that quarrel
        at my feet
Over an honor I can only guess at?
Can one ask the way of men considered to be dead
Who speak with an accent that resembles the accent of silence?
Center of the Earth! I am a living man.
These emperors, these kings, these prime ministers, listen
        to them as they offer me their services
Because I traffic at the surface with the stars and the daylight.
I come off best with the dead men and women and the dead
        little ones.
I say to them: "Look at this heart of mine,

Comme il bat dans ma poitrine et m'inonde de chaleur!
Il me fait un toit de chaume où grésille le soleil.
Approchez-vous pour l'entendre, vous en avez eu un pareil.
N'ayez pas peur, nous sommes ici dans l'intimité infernale."

Autour de moi, certains se poussent du coude,
Prétendent que j'ai l'éternité devant moi,
Que je puis bien rester une petite minute,
Que je ne serais pas là si je n'étais mort moi-même.
Pour toute réponse je repars
Puisqu'on m'attend toujours merveilleusement à l'autre bout
    du monde.
Mon coeur bourdonne, c'est une montre dont les aiguilles
    se hâtent comme les électrons
Et seul peut l'arrêter le regard de Dieu quand il pénètre
    dans le mécanisme.

Air pur, air des oiseaux, air bleu de la surface,
Je remonte vers toi!
Voici Jésus qui s'avance pour maçonner la voûte du ciel.
La Terre en passant frôle ses pieds avec les forêts les plus
    douces.
Depuis deux mille ans il l'a quittée pour visiter d'autres
    sphères,
Chaque Terre s'imagine être son unique maîtresse
Et lui prépare des guirlandes nuptiales de martyrs.
Jésus réveille en passant des astres morts qu'il secoue,
Comme des soldats profondément endormis.
Et les astres de tourner religieusement dans le ciel
En suppliant le Christ de tourner avec eux.
Mais lui repart, les pieds nus sur une aérienne Judée,
Et nombreux restent les astres prosternés
Dans la sidérale poussière.
Jésus, pourquoi te montrer si je ne crois pas encore?
Mon regard serait-il en avance sur mon âme?

Je ne suis pas homme à faire toujours les demandes et
    les réponses!

How it beats in my breast and floods me with heat!
It makes a thatched roof for me where the sun crackles.
Come close to hear it—you, too, have had one like it.
Don't be afraid, we're in infernal privacy here."

Around me, certain creatures are taunting me,
Maintaining that all eternity lies before me,
That I could easily stay for an instant,
That I would not be there if I were not dead myself.
As total answer I set off again
Seeing that I'm always being marvelously awaited at the other
    end of the world.
My heart hums, it's a watch whose hands hurry like electrons
And alone can stop the glance of God when He penetrates
    the mechanism.

Pure air, air of the birds, blue air of the surface,
I climb toward you again!
Here is Jesus who is moving to build up the vault of Heaven.
The Earth in passing brushes his feet with the softest forests.
For two thousand years he has left it to visit other spheres.
Each Earth imagines herself to be his only mistress
And prepares for him the nuptial garlands of martyrs.
Jesus wakes in passing some dead stars which he shakes
Like soldiers in a deep sleep.
And the stars revolve religiously in the sky
Imploring Christ to turn with them,
But he sets out again, barefoot in an aerial Judea.
And great numbers of the stars remain prostrated
In the astral dust.
Jesus, why are you turning up when I still don't believe?
Would my eyes be ahead of my soul?

I'm not the man to be always asking and answering!

Holà muchachos! J'entends crier des vivants dans des arbres
    chevelus,
Ces vivants sont mes enfants, échappés, radieux, de ma moëlle!
Un cheval m'attend attaché à un eucalyptus des pampas,
Il est temps que je rattrape son hennissement dans l'air dur,
Dans l'air qui a ses rochers, mais je suis seul à les voir!

Holà muchachos! I hear the living cry out in the hairy trees.
These living ones are my children, escaped, radiant,
　　of my own marrow!
A horse is waiting for me tied to a eucalyptus of the pampas,
It's time that I recapture its neighing in the hard air,
In the air which has its boulders, but I'm the only one
　　to see them!

1924

Le Forçat Innocent
1930

Ecoute, apprendras-tu à m'écouter de loin?

Ecoute, apprendras-tu à m'écouter de loin,
Il s'agit de pencher le coeur plus que l'oreille,
Tu trouveras en toi des ponts et des chemins
Pour venir jusqu'à moi qui regarde et qui veille.

Qu'importe en sa longueur l'Océan Atlantique,
Les champs, les bois, les monts qui sont entre nous deux?
L'un après l'autre un jour il faudra qu'ils abdiquent
Lorsque de ce côté tu tourneras les yeux.

Listen, Will You Learn To Hear Me From Afar?

Listen, will you learn to hear me from afar?
It's a question of inclining the heart more than the ear.
You'll find bridges in yourself and roads
To reach all the way to me who waits and stares.

What does it matter, the Atlantic's width,
The fields, woods, mountains between us two?
One by one they'll have to give up on that day
You turn your eyes this way.

Oloron-Sainte-Marie

à la mémoire de Rainer Maria Rilke

Comme du temps de mes pères les Pyrénées écoutent aux portes
Et je me sens surveillé par leurs rugueuses cohortes.
Le gave coule, paupières basses, ne voulant pas de différence
Entre les hommes et les ombres,
Et il passe entre des pierres
Qui ne craignent pas les siècles
Mais s'appuient dessus pour rêver.

C'est la ville de mon père, j'ai affaire un peu partout.
Je rôde dans les rues et monte des étages n'importe où,
Ces étages font de moi comme un sentier de montagne,
J'entre sans frapper dans des chambres que traverse la campagne,
Les miroirs refont les bois, portent secours aux ruisseaux,
Je me découvre dedans pris et repris par leurs eaux.
J'erre sur les toits d'ardoise, je vais en haut de la tour,
Et, pour rassembler les morts qu'une rumeur effarouche,
Je suis le battant humain,
Qui ne révèle aucun bruit,
De la cloche de la nuit,
Dans le ciel pyrénéen.

O morts à la démarche dérobée,
Que nous confondons toujours avec l'immobilité,
Perdus dans votre sourire comme sous la pluie l'épitaphe,
Morts aux postures contraintes et gênés par trop d'espace,
O vous qui venez rôder autour de nos positions,
C'est nous qui sommes les boiteux tout prêts à tomber sur
        le front.

Vous êtes guéris du sang
De ce sang qui nous assoiffe.

Vous êtes guéris de voir
La mer, le ciel et les bois.

Oloron-Sainte-Marie

to the memory of Rainer Maria Rilke

As in the times of my fathers, the Pyrenees listen at the doors
And I feel myself under the surveillance of their rough troops.
The mountain stream flows, eyelids lowered, not wanting
    a difference
Between men and shadows
And runs among the stones
Which don't fear the centuries
But lean on them to dream.

This is my father's town, I have things to do here and there,
I roam the streets and walk up flights no matter where.
These staircases make a kind of mountain path for me;
I walk without knocking into rooms crossed by the countryside;
The mirrors renew the woods, bring help to the rivulets,
I discover myself inside caught and caught again by their waters,
I wander over the slate roofs, I go to the top of the tower,
And to round up the dead who are scared off by a murmur
I become the human bell clapper
Of the bell of the night
Whom no sound betrays
In the sky of the Pyrenees.

Oh dead ones with the surreptitious gait
That we always confound with motionlessness,
Lost in your smile like an epitaph under rain,
Dead ones with constrained postures, bothered by too much
    space,
Oh you who come to roam around our positions
It is we who are the lame ones all ready to stumble on our faces.

You are cured of blood,
Of this blood which makes us thirsty.

You are cured of seeing
The sea, the sky and the woods.

Vous en avez fini avec les lèvres, leurs raisons et leurs baisers,
Avec nos mains qui nous suivent partout sans nous apaiser,
Avec les cheveux qui poussent et les ongles qui se cassent,
Et, derrière le front dur, notre esprit qui se déplace.

Mais en nous rien n'est plus vrai
Que ce froid qui vous ressemble,

Nous ne sommes séparés
Que par le frisson d'un tremble.

Ne me tournez pas le dos. Devinez-vous
Un vivant de votre race près de vos anciens genoux?

Amis, ne craignez pas tant
Qu'on vous tire par un pan de votre costume flottant!

N'avez-vous pas un peu envie,
Chers écoliers de la mort, qu'on vous décline la vie?

Nous vous dirons de nouveau
Comment l'ombre et le soleil
Dans un instant qui sommeille,
Font et défont un bouleau.

Et nous vous reconstruirons
Chaque ville avec les arches respirantes de ses ponts,
La campagne avec le vent,
Et le soleil au milieu de ses frères se levant.

Etes-vous sûrs, êtes-vous sûrs de n'avoir rien à ajouter,
Que c'est toujours de ce côté le même jour, le même été?
Ah comment apaiser mes os dans leur misère,
Troupe blafarde, aveugle, au visage calcaire,
Qui réclame la mort de son chef aux yeux bleus
Tourné vers le dehors.

You have finished with the lips, their reasons and their kisses,
With our hands which follow us everywhere without soothing us,
With the hairs that grow and the nails that break,
And, behind the stony brow, our mind that thrusts.

But in us nothing is truer
Than this cold which resembles you,
We are separated
Only by the shiver of an aspen.

Don't turn your back on me. Do you sense
A living person of your race near your ancient knees?

Friends, don't be so afraid
That someone will pull you by a piece of your oversized
      costume!

Aren't you a little hopeful,
Dear schoolboys of death, that life will be declined for you
      like a noun?

We shall tell you again
How the shadow and the sun
In a moment of slumber
Make and remake a silver birch.

And we shall rebuild each town for you
With the breathing arches of its bridges,
The countryside with the wind
And the sun rising in the midst of its brothers.

Are you sure, are you sure that you have nothing to add,
That always from this side it's the same day, the same summer?
Ah, how pacify my bones in their misery,
Pale troop, blind, chalky-faced,
Who call for the death of their chief with the blue eyes
Turned toward the outdoors?

Je les entends qui m'emplissent de leur voix sourde,
Planté dans ma chair, ces os,
Comme de secrets couteaux
Qui n'ont jamais vu le jour :

"N'échappe pas ainsi à notre entendement.
Ton silence nous ment.
Nous ne faisons qu'un avec toi,
Ne nous oublie pas.

Nous avons partie liée,
Tels l'époux et l'épousée
Quand il souffle la bougie
Pour la longueur de la nuit."

"Petits os, grands os, cartilages,
Il est de plus cruelles cages.
Patientez, violents éclairs,
Dans l'orage clos de ma chair.

Thorax, sans arrière-pensée
Laisse entrer l'air de la croisée.
Comprendras-tu que le soleil
Va jusqu'à toi du fond du ciel?

Ecoute-moi, sombre humérus,
Les ténèbres de chair sont douces.
Il ne faut pas songer encor
A la flûte lisse des morts.

Et toi, rosaire d'os, colonne vertébrale,
Que nulle main n'égrènera,
Retarde notre heure ennemie,
Prions pour le ruisseau de vie
Qui se presse vers nos prunelles."

I hear them as they fill me with their muffled voices,
Planted in my flesh, these bones,
Like secret knives
That have never seen day:

"Don't slip away from our comprehension,
Your silence lies to us.
Only with you do we become one,
Don't forget us.

We are hand in glove
Like the bridegroom and the bride
When he blows out the candle
For the length of the night."

"Little bones, big bones, cartilages,
There are crueler cages.
Be patient, violent lightnings,
In the tempest of my flesh.

Thorax, without ulterior motives
Let in the air of the crossroads.
Will you understand that the sun
Comes from the far end of the sky
        all the way down to you?

Listen to me, sombre humerus,
The flesh gloom is sweet.
You mustn't dream any more
Of the smooth slender legs of the dead.

And you, rosary of bone, spinal column,
Whose beads no hand will tell,
Delay our enemy hour,
Let us pray for the rivulet of life
That presses against the pupils of our eyes."

Whisper in Agony

Ne vous étonnez pas,
Abaissez les paupières
Jusqu'à ce qu'elles soient
De veritable pierre.

Laissez faire le coeur,
Et même s'il s'arrête.
Il bat pour lui tout seul
Sur sa pente secrète.

Les mains s'allongeront
Dans leur barque de glace,
Et le front sera nu
Comme une grande place
Vide, entre deux armées.

Whisper in Agony

Don't be amazed,
Close your eyelids
Until they turn
Into real stone.

Leave your heart alone
Even if it stops.
It beats only for itself
On its secret slope.

Your hands will stretch out
In their barge of ice
And your brow will be bare
Like a great empty square
Between two hosts.

Le soleil parle bas

Le soleil parle bas
A la neige et l'engage
A mourir sans souffrir
Comme fait le nuage.

Quelle est cette autre voix
Qui me parle et m'engage?
Même au fort de l'hiver.
Serait-ce la chaleur
Qui fait tourner la Terre
Toujours d'un même coeur,
Et, pour me rassurer,
Dans toutes les saisons
Se penche à mon oreille
Et murmure mon nom?

The Sun Speaks Softly

The sun speaks softly
To the snow and pledges it
To die without suffering
As the cloud does.

What is that other voice
That speaks to me and pledges me?
Even in the depths of winter.
Would it be the heat
That makes the Earth turn
Always with the same will
And, to reassure me,
Leans into my ear
In all seasons
And murmurs my name?

Les Amis Inconnus
1934

L'allée

—Ne touchez pas l'épaule
Du cavalier qui passe,
Il se retournerait
Et ce serait la nuit,
Une nuit sans étoiles,
Sans courbe ni nuages.
—Alors que deviendrait
Tout ce qui fait le ciel,
La lune et son passage,
Et le bruit du soleil?
—Il vous faudrait attendre
Qu'un second cavalier
Aussi puissant que l'autre
Consentit à passer.

The Lane

"Don't touch the shoulder
Of the horseman passing by,
He would turn his head
And it would be night,
A night without stars,
Without curve or clouds."
　　"Then what would become
　　Of all that makes the sky,
　　The moon and her path
　　And the sound of the sun?"
"You would have to wait
Until a second horseman
As powerful as the first
Might consent to pass by."

Il couchait seul dans de grands lits
De hautes herbes et d'orties,
Son corps nu toujours éclairé
Dans les défilés de la nuit
Par un soleil encore violent
Qui venait d'un siècle passé
Par monts et par vaux de lumière
A travers mille obscurités.
Quand il avançait sur les routes
Il ne se retournait jamais.
C'était l'affaire de son double
Toujours à la bonne distance
Et qui lui servait d'écuyer.
Quelquefois les astres hostiles
Pour s'assurer que c'était eux
Les éprouvaient d'un cent de flèches
Patiemment empoisonnées.
Quand ils passaient, même les arbres
Etaient pris de vivacité,
Les troncs frissonnaient dans la fibre,
Visiblement réfléchissaient.
Et ne parlons pas du feuillage,
Toujours une feuille en tombait
Même au printemps quand elles tiennent
Et sont dures de volonté.
Les insectes se dépêchaient
Dans leur besogne quotidienne,
Tous, la tête dans les épaules,
Comme s'ils se la reprochaient.
La pierre prenait conscience
De ses anciennes libertés;
Lui, savait ce qui se passait
Derrière l'immobilité
Et devant la fragilité.
Les jeunes filles le craignaient,

The Stranger Among Us

He slept alone in large beds
Of high grass and nettles,
His naked body constantly illuminated
In the gorges of the night
By a still fierce sun
Which came from a bygone century
Through mountains and valleys of light
Across a thousand glooms.
When he moved along the roads
He never looked back.
That was the business of his double,
Always at a good distance,
Who served him as escort.
Sometimes the hostile stars
To make sure it was really them
Afflicted them with a hundred arrows
Patiently poisoned.
When they passed by, even the trees
Were seized with animation,
Their trunks trembling in their fibre,
Visibly reflected,
Not to speak of the foliage
Where a leaf would always fall
Even in the spring when they hold fast
And are hard of will.
The insects would hurry
As they went about their daily tasks,
All with heads sunk in their shoulders
As though they reproached themselves for working.
The stone was becoming conscious
Of its ancient liberties;
The stranger knew what was taking place
Behind its motionlessness
And before the fragility of everything else.
The young girls were afraid of him;

Parfois des femmes l'appelaient
Mais il n'en regardait aucune
Dans sa cruelle chasteté.
Les murs excitaient son esprit,
Il s'en éloignait enrichi
Par une gerbe de secrets
Volés au milieu de leur nuit
Et que toujours il recélait
Dans son coeur sûr, son seul bagage,
Avec le coeur de l'écuyer.
Ses travaux de terrassement
Dans les carrières de son âme
Le surprenaient-ils, harassé,
Près de bornes sans inscription,
Tirant une langue sanglante
Tel un chien aux poumons crevés,
Qu'il regardait ses longues mains
Comme un miroir de chair et d'os
Et aussitôt il repartait.
Ses enjambées étaient célèbres,
Mais seul il connaissait son nom
Que voici: "Plus grave que l'homme
Et savant comme certains morts
Qui n'ont jamais pu s'endormir."

Sometimes women called out to him
But he never looked at any of them
In his cruel chastity.
Walls excited his imagination;
He would move away enriched
By a sheaf of secrets
Stolen in the middle of their night
And which he always harbored
In his firm heart, his only baggage,
With the heart of his escort.
His works of excavation
In the quarries of his soul
Surprised him and wearied him,
Passing milestones without inscription,
Sticking out his bloody tongue
Like a dog with punctured lungs,
Looking at his long hands
Like a mirror of flesh and bone,
Starting off again forthwith.
His strides were famous,
But he alone knew his name,
Which is: "More solemn than man
And learned like certain dead men
Who have never been able to fall asleep."

Les mains photographiées

On les faisait pénétrer au monde des surfaces lisses,
Où même des montagnes rocheuses sont douces, faciles
    au toucher,
Et tiennent dans le creux de la main.
On les traitait comme un visage pour la première fois de
    leur vie,
Et sous les feux des projecteurs
Elles se sentirent un front vague
Et les symptômes premiers d'une naissante physionomie.
De très loin venait la mémoire aborder ces rivages vierges
Avec le calme d'une houle qui mit longtemps à se former.
Les connaissances du cerveau parvenaient enfin jusqu'au pouce.
Le pouce légèrement acquiesçait dans son domaine,
Et pendant que dura la pose
Les mains donnèrent leur nom au soleil, à la belle journée.
Elles appelèrent "tremblement" cette légère hésitation
Qui leur venait du coeur humain, à l'autre bout des veines
    chaudes,
Elles comprirent que la vie est chose passante et fragile.
Puis, les projecteurs s'éloignant,
Elles ne connurent plus rien de ce qu'elles avaient deviné
Durant ce court entretien avec des forces lumineuses.
Le moment était arrivé où l'on ne pouvait même plus,
Les appeler oublieuses.

The Photographed Hands

They were being made to penetrate the world of smooth surfaces
Where even rocky mountains are soft, easy to the touch
And are held in the hollow of the hand.
They were being treated like a face for the first time in their
    lives
And in the glare of the floodlights
They sensed a vague brow in themselves
And the first symptoms of a nascent physiognomy.
From very far off memory was moving to approach these
    virgin shores
With the calm of a swell that takes a long time to shape itself.
The consciousness of the brain was finally reaching down
    to the thumb,
The thumb was lightly acquiescing in its domain
And while the exposure lasted
The hands gave their name to the sun, to the lovely day.
They called this gentle hesitation, "trembling,"
Which came to them from the human heart at the other end
    of the hot veins.
They understood that life was a passing and fragile thing.
Afterwards, the floodlights having moved away,
They remembered nothing of what they had guessed
During their short interview with the luminous forces.
The moment had arrived when one could no longer
Call the hands forgetful.

L'aube dans la chambre

Le petit jour vient toucher une tête en son sommeil,
Il glisse sur l'os frontal
Et s'assure que c'est bien le même homme que la veille.
A pas de loup, les couleurs pénètrent par la croisée
Avec leur longue habitude de ne pas faire de bruit.
La blanche vient de Timor et toucha la Palestine
Et voilà que sur le lit elle s'incline et s'étale.
Cette grise, avec regret se sépara de la Chine,
La voici sur le miroir
Lui donnant sa profondeur,
Rien qu'en s'approchant de lui.
Une autre va vers l'armoire et la frotte un peu de jaune;
Celle-ci repeint de noir
La condition de l'homme
Qui repose dans son lit.
Alors l'âme qui le sait,
Mère inquiète toujours près de ce corps qui s'allonge:
"Le malheur n'est pas sur nous
Puisque le corps de nos jours
Dans la pénombre respire.
Il n'est plus grande douleur
Que ne plus pouvoir souffrir
Et que l'âme soit sans gîte
Devant des portes fermées.
Un jour je serai privée de ce grand corps près de moi;
J'aime bien à deviner ses formes dessous les draps,
Mon ami le sang qui coule dans son delta malaisé,
Et cette main qui parfois
Bouge un peu sous quelque songe
Qui ne laissera de trace
Dans le corps ni dans son âme.
Mais il dort, ne pensons pas pour ne pas le réveiller.
Qu'on ne m'entende pas plus que le feuillage qui pousse
Ni la rose de verdure."

Dawn in the Room

The first light is just touching a head in its sleep—
It glides on the frontal bone
And assures itself that it's really the same man as the day before.
Stealthily, the colors creep through the window
With their longtime habit of making no noise.
The white comes from Timor and touched Palestine—
See how it leans over the bed and spreads out.
This grey parted from China regretfully—
Here it is on the mirror
Giving it its depth
Merely by coming closer.
Another moves toward the wardrobe and rubs it with a bit of
      yellow.
This one repaints with black
The condition of the man
Lying in his bed.
Then the soul speaks who understands him,
Anxious mother always hovering near his outstretched body:
"Misfortune is not upon us
As long as this body whose days I share
Breathes in the half-light.
It's no great sorrow
To be unable to suffer anymore
Or that the soul might stand without shelter
Before locked doors.
Someday, I'll be deprived of this great near body;
I like to fathom its shapes under the sheets,
My friend, the blood, flowing in his difficult delta
And this hand which sometimes
Shifts a little beneath some dream
That leaves no trace
In the body or the soul.
But he's sleeping, let's not think or we'll wake him.
Let my voice be no louder than the thrusting foliage
Or the greenery rose."

Le regret de la terre

Un jour, quand nous dirons: "C'était le temps du soleil,
Vous souvenez-vous, il éclairait la moindre ramille
Et aussi bien la femme âgée que la jeune fille étonnée,
Il savait donner leur couleur aux objets dès qu'il se posait.
Il suivait le cheval coureur et s'arrêtait avec lui.
C'était le temps inoubliable où nous étions sur la Terre,
Où cela faisait du bruit de faire tomber quelque chose,
Nous regardions alentour avec nos yeux connaisseurs,
Nos oreilles comprenaient toutes les nuances de l'air,
Et lorsque le pas de l'ami s'avançait, nous le savions;
Nous ramassions aussi bien une fleur qu'un caillou poli,
Le temps où nous ne pouvions attraper la fumée,
Ah! c'est tout ce que nos mains sauraient saisir maintenant."

Longing for the Earth

Someday, we'll say, "It was the time of the sun,
Remember, he used to shine on the least twig,
On the aged woman as well as the astonished young one.
He would know how to give objects their color
     as soon as he lighted on them.
He would run with the racehorse and halt with him, too.
It was the unforgettable time when we were all on Earth,
Where a noise was made if we dropped something.
We used to look around with the eyes of connoisseurs,
Our ears would comprehend all the nuances of the air
And when the step of a friend drew near we knew it.
We would as easily pick up a flower as a polished pebble,
That time when we were powerless to catch smoke.
Ah, smoke is all that our hands would know how to seize
    these days!"

La demeure entourée

Le corps de la montagne hésite à ma fenêtre:
"Comment peut-on entrer si l'on est la montagne,
Si l'on est en hauteur, avec roches, cailloux,
Un morceau de la Terre, altéré par le Ciel?"
Le feuillage des bois entoure ma maison:
"Les bois ont-ils leur mot à dire là-dedans?
Notre monde branchu, notre monde feuillu
Que peut-il dans la chambre où siège ce lit blanc,
Près de ce chandelier qui brûle par le haut,
Et devant cette fleur qui trempe dans un verre?
Que peut-il pour cet homme et son bras replié,
Cette main écrivant entre ces quatres murs?
Prenons avis de nos racines délicates,
Il ne nous a pas vus, il cherche au fond de lui
Des arbres différents qui comprennent sa langue."
Et la rivière dit: "Je ne veux rien savoir,
Je coule pour moi seule et j'ignore les hommes.
Je ne suis jamais là où l'on croit me trouver
Et vais me devançant, crainte de m'attarder.
Tant pis pour ces gens-là qui s'en vont sur leurs jambes.
Ils partent, et toujours reviennent sur leurs pas."
Mais l'étoile se dit: "Je tremble au bout d'un fil.
Si nul ne pense à moi je cesse d'exister."

Home Surrounded

The hulk of the mountain hesitates at my window:
"How can you get in if you're a mountain,
If you're way up there, with boulders and pebbles,
A bit of the Earth that's troubled by Heaven?"
The green of the woods surrounds my house:
"Do the woods have their say inside?
Our branchy world, our leafy world,
What can it do in that room where the white bed lies
Near the candlestick burning high
In front of the flower that steeps in a glass?
What can it do for that man who leans on his arm,
That hand which writes among the four walls?
Let's take the advice of our delicate roots,
The man hasn't seen us, he's searching his depths
For various trees that fathom his tongue."
And the river says, "I don't want to hear a thing,
I flow for myself alone and know nothing of men.
I'm never where you expect to find me,
I rush and outrun myself, afraid of loitering.
Never mind those people who run off on their legs,
They leave and always come back to retrace their steps."
But the star says to itself, "I tremble at the end of
    a thread,
If no one thinks of me I cease to exist."

Naufrage

Une table tout près, une lampe très loin
Qui dans l'air irrité ne peuvent se rejoindre,
Et jusqu'à l'horizon une plage déserte.
Un homme à la mer lève un bras, crie: "Au secours!"
Et l'écho lui répond: "Qu'entendez-vous par là?"

Shipwreck

A table quite near, a lamp very far
That can't be joined again in the angry air,
And as far as the horizon a deserted beach.
A man in the sea is waving and screaming, "Help!"
And the echo is replying, "What do you mean by that?"

Visite de la nuit

Terrasse où balcon, je posai le pied
A la place exacte où l'on sait toute chose,

J'attendis longtemps, gêné par mon corps,
Il faisait grand jour et l'on approchait.

C'était bien la Nuit convertie en femme,
Tremblante au soleil comme une perdrix,

Si peu faite encore à son enveloppe
Toute errante en soi, même dans son coeur.

Quand il m'arrivait de faire des signes
Elle regardait mais voyait ailleurs.

Je ne bougeais plus pour mieux la convaincre
Mais aucun silence ne lui parvenait.

Ses gestes obscurs comme ses murmures
Toujours me voulaient d'un autre côté.

Quand baissa le jour, d'un pas très humain
A jamais déçu, elle s'éloigna.

Elle rejoignit au bout de la rue
Son vertige ardent, sa forme espacée.

Comme chaque nuit elle s'étoila
De ses milliers d'yeux dont aucun ne voit.

Et depuis ce jour je cède à mes ombres.

Visit of Night

Terrace or balcony, I placed my foot
In the exact spot where one knows everything.

I waited a long time, held back by my body.
It was almost broad daylight and someone was coming.

It was Night herself turned into a woman,
Trembling in the sun like a partridge,

Still ill at ease with her appearance,
Wandering about in herself and in her heart.

When I would make a sign to her
She would stare back but was looking elsewhere.

To better persuade her, I didn't stir again,
But not even silence reached her.

Her dark gestures like her murmurings
Approached me from every side.

When day declined she went away
With a very human step, deceived forever.

She turned up again at the end of the street,
Her vertigo intense, her shape spaced out.

As in each night, she starred herself
With her thousands of eyes, all blind.

And since that day I yield to my shadows.

La Fable du Monde
1938

La goutte de pluie

(Dieu Parle)

Je cherche une goutte de pluie
Qui vient de tomber dans la mer.
Dans sa rapide verticale
Elle luisait plus que les autres
Car seule entre les autres gouttes
Elle eut la force de comprendre
Que, très douce dans l'eau salée,
Elle allait se perdre à jamais.
Alors je cherche dans la mer
Et sur les vagues, alertées,
Je cherche pour faire plaisir
A ce fragile souvenir
Dont je suis seul dépositaire.
Mais j'ai beau faire, il est des choses
Où Dieu même ne peut plus rien
Malgré sa bonne volonté
Et l'assistance sans paroles
Du ciel, des vagues et de l'air.

The Drop of Rain

(GOD SPEAKS)

I am looking for a drop of rain
Which has just fallen into the sea.
In its rapid descent
It glistened more than the others
Because alone among the other drops
It had the strength to understand
That sweetly in the salty water
It was going to lose itself forever.
So I am searching the sea
And alerting the waves.
I am searching in order to please
That fragile memory
Of which I am the sole guardian.
But it's no use, there are some things
Which God Himself cannot do
Despite His good will
And the speechless assistance
Of the sky, the waves and the air.

Prière à l'inconnu

Voilà que je me surprends à t'adresser la parole,
Mon Dieu, moi qui ne sais encore si tu existes,
Et ne comprends pas la langue de tes églises chuchotantes,
Je regarde les autels, la voûte de ta maison
Comme qui dit simplement : "Voilà du bois, de la pierre,
Voilà des colonnes romanes, il manque le nez à ce saint
Et au dedans comme au dehors il y a la détresse humaine."
Je baisse les yeux sans pouvoir m'agenouiller pendant la messe
Comme si je laissais passer l'orage au-dessus de ma tête
Et je ne puis m'empêcher de penser à autre chose.
Hélas j'aurai passé ma vie à penser à autre chose.
Cette autre chose c'est encore moi, c'est peut-être mon vrai
    moi-même.
C'est là que je me réfugie, c'est peut-être là que tu es,
Je n'aurai jamais vécu que dans ces lointains attirants,
Le moment présent est un cadeau dont je n'ai pas su profiter,
Je n'en connais pas bien l'usage, je le tourne dans tous les sens,
Sans savoir faire marcher sa mécanique difficile.
Mon Dieu, je ne crois pas en toi, je voudrais te parler
    tout de même ;
J'ai bien parlé aux étoiles bien que je les sache sans vie,
Aux plus humbles des animaux quand je les savais sans réponse,
Aux arbres qui, sans le vent, seraient muets comme la tombe.
Je me suis parlé à moi-même quand je ne sais pas bien si j'existe.
Je ne sais si tu entends nos prières à nous les hommes,
Je ne sais si tu as envie de les écouter,
Si tu as comme nous un coeur qui est toujours sur le qui-vive,
Et des oreilles ouvertes aux nouvelles les plus différentes.
Je ne sais pas si tu aimes à regarder par ici,
Pourtant je voudrais te remettre en mémoire la planète Terre,
Avec ses fleurs, ses cailloux, ses jardins et ses maisons,
Avec tous les autres et nous qui savons bien que nous souffrons.

Prayer to the Unknown

Behold how I surprise myself by addressing a word to you,
My God, I who still don't know if you exist
And don't understand the language of your whispering churches.
I look at the altars, the vault of your house
As one who says simply, "Over there is wood and stone,
There are Roman columns, the nose of this saint is missing
And inside as outside there is human distress."
I close my eyes, unable to kneel during mass
As if I were allowing a storm to pass over my head
And I can't stop myself from thinking of something else.
Alas, I shall have passed my whole life thinking of
     something else
And this other thing, it's still me, it's perhaps my true self.
It's there that I take refuge, it's perhaps there that you are,
I shall never have lived except in these appealing distances,
The present moment is a gift I haven't known how to profit by,
I'm not very well acquainted with the use of it, I turn it
     this way and that
Without knowing how to make its difficult mechanism work.
My God, I don't believe in you, but I'd like to speak with you
     all the same;
I've spoken to the stars although I know them to be lifeless,
To the humblest of animals when I knew them unable
     to answer,
To the trees who, without the wind, would be mute as
     the tomb.
I've been talking to myself when I really don't know if I exist.
I don't know if you hear our prayers, the prayers of mankind,
I don't know if you desire to hear them,
If you have a heart like us which is always on the alert
And ears open to the most varied news.
I don't know if you care to look down here,
Yet I'd like to put the planet Earth back in your memory
With its flowers, its pebbles, its gardens and its houses,
With all the others and with us who know well enough that
     we suffer.

Je veux t'adresser sans tarder ces humbles paroles humaines
Parce qu'il faut que chacun tente à présent tout l'impossible,
Même si tu n'es qu'un souffle d'il y a des milliers d'années,
Une grande vitesse acquise, une durable mélancolie
Qui ferait tourner encore les sphères dans leur mélodie.
Je voudrais, mon Dieu sans visage et peut-être sans espérance,
Attirer ton attention, parmi tant de ciels, vagabonde,
Sur les hommes qui n'ont plus de repos sur la planète.
Ecoute-moi, cela presse, ils vont tous se décourager
Et l'on ne va plus reconnaître les jeunes parmi les âgés.
Chaque matin ils se demandent si la tuerie va commencer,
De tous côtés l'on prépare de bizarres distributeurs
De sang, de plaintes et de larmes,
L'on se demande si les blés ne cachent pas déjà des fusils.
Le temps serait-il passé où tu occupais des hommes,
T'appelle-t-on dans d'autres mondes, médecin en consultation,
Ne sachant où donner de la tête, laissant mourir sa clientèle.
Ecoute-moi, je ne suis qu'un homme parmi tant d'autres,
L'âme se plaît dans notre corps, ne demande pas à s'enfuir
Dans un éclatement de bombe,
Elle est pour nous une caresse, une secrète flatterie.
Laisse-nous respirer encor sans songer aux nouveaux poisons,
Laisse-nous regarder nos enfants sans penser tout le temps
        à la mort.
Nous n'avons pas du tout le coeur aux batailles, aux généraux.
Laisse-nous notre va-et-vient comme un troupeaux dans ses
        sonnailles,
Une odeur de lait se mêlant à l'odeur de l'herbe grasse.
Ah! si tu existes, mon Dieu, regarde de notre côté,
Viens te délasser parmi nous, la Terre est belle avec ses arbres,
Ses fleuves et ses étangs, si belle que l'on dirait
Que tu la regrettes un peu.
Mon Dieu, ne va pas faire encore la sourde oreille,
Et ne va pas m'en vouloir si nous sommes à tu et à toi,

I want to address you without delay with these humble
    human words,
Because it's necessary now that each one of us attempts the
    wholly impossible,
Even if you're only a breath out of thousands of years,
A great moment, a durable melancholy
Which would make the spheres turn again in their melody.
I'd like, my faceless and perhaps hopeless God,
To attract your attention wandering among so many skies
Onto men, who can no longer rest on this planet.
Listen to me, it's urgent, they're all going to lose heart
And one won't be able to tell the young from the old anymore.
Each morning people wonder if the slaughter is going to begin,
Everywhere strange dispensers are being prepared
Of blood, of groans and of tears.
One asks oneself if the wheat isn't already concealing rifles.
Has the time gone when you occupied yourself with men?
Do you call yourself consulting physician in other worlds,
Not knowing which way to turn, letting your patients die?
Listen to me, I'm only one man among many,
The soul likes to be in our bodies, don't ask it to fly off
In a bomb explosion,
She is a caress for us, a secret flattery.
Allow us to continue breathing without dreaming of
    new poisons,
Allow us to look at our children without thinking of death
    all the time.
We absolutely don't have the heart for battles or for generals.
Allow us our comings and goings like a belled herd,
An odor of milk mixing with the odor of rich grass.
Ah, if you exist, my God, take a look in our direction,
Come refresh yourself among us, the Earth is beautiful
    with its trees,
Its rivers and its ponds, so beautiful that it would seem
That you must miss it a little.
My God, don't keep turning a deaf ear on us
And don't be angry with me if I'm too familiar with you,

Si je te parle avec tant d'abrupte simplicité,
Je croirais moins qu'en tout autre en un Dieu qui terrorise;
Plus que par la foudre tu sais t'exprimer par les brins d'herbe,
Et par les yeux des ruisseaux et par les jeux des enfants,
Ce qui n'empêche pas les mers et les chaînes de montagnes.
Tu ne peux pas m'en vouloir de dire ce que je pense,
De réfléchir comme je peux sur l'homme et sur son existence,
Avec la franchise de la Terre et des diverses saisons
(Et peut-être de toi-même dont j'ignorerais les leçons).
Je ne suis pas sans excuses, veuille accepter mes pauvres ruses,
Tant de choses se préparent sournoisement contre nous,
Quoique nous fassions nous craignons d'être pris au dépourvu,
Et d'être comme le taureau qui ne comprend pas ce qui se passe,
Le mène-t-on à l'abattoir, il ne sait où il va comme ça,
Et juste avant de recevoir le coup de mort sur le front
Il se répète qu'il a faim et brouterait résolument,
Mais qu'est-ce qu'ils ont ce matin avec leur tablier plein
        de sang
A vouloir tous s'occuper de lui?

(Pontigny, Juillet 1937.)

If I speak to you with so much abrupt simplicity,
I'd believe least in a God who terrorizes.
More than by lightning you know how to express yourself
    by the blades of grass
And by the eyes of streams and by the games of children,
Not to mention the seas and the mountain chains.
You can't hold it against me if I say what I think,
To reflect as I can on man and his existence
With the frankness of the Earth and the various seasons
(And perhaps of yourself whose lessons I'm not unaware of).
I'm not without excuses, please accept my poor stratagems,
So many things are being deceitfully prepared against us.
No matter what we may do we're afraid of being caught
    off guard
And to be like the bull who doesn't understand what's
    happening to him
As they lead him to the abattoir, not knowing where he's going
And just before receiving the death blow on his frontal bone
He repeats to himself that he's hungry and would happily graze,
But what's the matter with them this morning with their
    aprons full of blood
And everyone wanting to bother with him?

                                        Pontigny, July 1937

Le corps

Ici l'univers est à l'abri dans la profonde température
    de l'homme
Et les étoiles délicates avancent de leurs pas célestes
Dans l'obscurité qui fait loi dès que la peau est franchie,
Ici tout s'accompagne des pas silencieux de notre sang
Et de secrètes avalanches qui ne font aucun bruit dans nos
    parages,
Ici le contenu est tellement plus grand
Que le corps à l'étroit, le triste contenant...
Mais cela n'empêche pas nos humbles mains de tous les jours
De toucher les différents points de notre corps qui loge
    les astres,
Avec les distances interstellaires en nous fidèlement
    respectées
Comme des géants infinis réduits à la petitesse par le corps
    humain, où il nous faut tenir tant bien que mal,
Nous passons les uns près des autres, cachant mal nos étoiles,
    nos vertiges,
Qui se reflètent dans nos yeux, seules fêlures de notre peau.
Et nous sommes toujours sous le coup de cette immensité
    intérieure
Même quand notre monde, frappé de doute,
Recule en nous rapidement jusqu'à devenir minuscule
    et s'effacer,
Notre coeur ne battant plus que pour sa pelure de chair,
Réduits que nous sommes alors à l'extrême nudité de
    nos organes,
Ces bêtes à l'abandon dans leur sanglante écurie.

The Body

Here the universe is sheltered in the profound temperature of man
And the delicate stars advance with their celestial pacings
In the darkness which has been law since the skin was
    surmounted.
Here everything accompanies the silent steps of our blood
And of secret avalanches noiseless in our latitudes.
Here the contents are so much larger
Than the cramped body, the sad container...
But that doesn't stop our humble everyday hands
From touching the various points of this body of ours that
    accommodates the stars,
With the interstellar distances faithfully respected in us.
Like infinite giants reduced to littleness by the human body,
    in which we must hold as much good as evil,
We pass each other by, barely hiding our stars, our vertigoes,
Which are reflected in our eyes, unique fissures of our skin,
And we are always under the influence of this interior immensity
Even when our world, stricken with doubt,
Recoils in us rapidly to the point of tininess and erases itself,
Our heart beating only for its peel of flesh,
Reduced as we then are to the extreme nudity of our organs,
Those neglected beasts in their bloody stables.

Beau monstre de la nuit, palpitant de ténèbres

"Beau monstre de la nuit, palpitant de ténèbres,
Vous montrez un museau humide d'outre-ciel,
Vous approchez de moi, vous me tendez la patte
Et vous la retirez comme pris d'un soupçon.
Pourtant je suis l'ami de vos gestes obscurs,
Mes yeux touchent le fond de vos sourdes fourrures.
Ne verrez-vous en moi un frère ténébreux
Dans ce monde où je suis bourgeois de l'autre monde,
Gardant par devers moi ma plus claire chanson.
Allez, je sais aussi les affres du silence
Avec mon coeur hâtif, usé de patience,
Qui frappe sans réponse aux portes de la mort.
—Mais la mort te répond par des intermittences
Quand ton coeur effrayé se cogne à la cloison,
Et tu n'es que d'un monde où l'on craint de mourir."
Et les yeux dans les yeux, à petits reculons,
Le monstre s'éloigna dans l'ombre téméraire,
Et tout le ciel, comme à l'ordinaire, s'étoila.

Beautiful Monster of the Night

"Beautiful monster of the night, throbbing with darkness,
You display a muzzle damp from outer space,
You approach me, you offer me your paw
And pull it back as though seized with suspicion.
Nevertheless, I am the friend of your dark gestures,
My eyes plumb the depths of your muted coat.
Won't you view me as a brother in darkness
In this world where I'm really a citizen of the next world,
Keeping for myself my purest song.
Go, I also know the pangs of silence
With my hasty heart, worn-out with patience,
Knocking unanswered at the doors of death."
"But death answers you from time to time
When your frightened heart beats against its walls,
And you're from a world where they're afraid to die."
And eye to eye, with little backward steps,
The monster withdrew into the reckless dark
And the sky, as always, studded itself with stars.

L'enfant et les escaliers

Toi que j'entends courir dans les escaliers de la maison
Et qui me caches ton visage et même le reste du corps,
Lorsque je me montre à la rampe,
N'es-tu pas mon enfance qui fréquente les lieux de ma
    préférence,
Toi qui t'éloignes difficilement de ton ancien locataire.
Je te devine à ta façon pour ainsi dire invisible
De rôder autour de moi lorsque nul ne nous regarde
Et de t'enfuir comme quelqu'un qu'on ne doit pas voir
    avec un autre.
Fort bien, je ne dirai pas que j'ai pu te reconnaître,
Mais garde aussi notre secret, rumeur cent fois familière
De petits pas anciens dans les escaliers d'à présent.

The Child and the Stairs

You whom I hear running up and down the stairs of the house
Hiding your face from me and even the rest of yourself
When I come to the banister,
Aren't you my childhood frequenting my favorite places,
You who move away with difficulty from your former tenant?
I recognize who you are because of your invisible way,
    so to speak,
Of prowling around me when no one is watching
And running away like someone who ought not to be seen
    with another.
Very well, I won't say that I've been able to recognize you,
But you must also keep our secret, low sound a hundred times
    familiar
Of little former steps on the present-day stairs.

L'enfant et la rivière

De sa rive l'enfance
Nous regarde couler :
"Quelle est cette rivière
Où mes pieds sont mouillés,
Ces barques agrandies,
Ces reflets dévoilés,
Cette confusion
Où je me reconnais,
Quelle est cette façon
D'être et d'avoir été ?"

Et moi qui ne peux pas répondre
Je me fais songe pour passer aux pieds d'une ombre.

The Child and the River

From his riverbank
Childhood watches us flowing:
"What is this river
Where my feet get wet,
These magnified boats,
These unveiled reflections,
This confusion
Where I recognize myself,
What is this business
Of being and of having been?"

And I who cannot reply
Turn myself into a dream
In order to pass by
The feet of a shadow.

C'est vous quand vous êtes partie

C'est vous quand vous êtes partie,
L'air peu à peu qui se referme
Mais toujours prêt à se rouvrir
Dans sa tremblante cicatrice,
Et c'est mon âme à contre-jour
Si profondément étourdie
De ce brusque manque d'amour
Qu'elle n'en trouve plus sa forme
Entre la douleur et l'oubli.
Et c'est mon coeur mal protégé
Par un peu de chair et tant d'ombre
Qui se fait au goût de la tombe
Dans ce rien de jour étouffé
Tombant des astres, goutte à goutte,
Miel secret de ce qui n'est plus
Qu'un peu de rêve révolu.

It's You When You Have Left

It's you when you have left,
The air closing up bit by bit
But always ready to open afresh
In its quivering scar,
And it's my soul against the light
So profoundly dazed
At this abrupt lack of love
That it no longer finds its shape
Between the pain and the forgetting.
And it's my heart, poorly shielded
By a little flesh and so much darkness,
Which becomes used to the taste
        of the tomb
In this nothing of extinguished day
Falling from the stars, drop by drop,
Secret honey
Of what is no more
Than a bit of bygone dream.

Visages des animaux

Visages des animaux
Si bien modelés du dedans à cause de tous les mots que vous
    n'avez pas su dire,
Tant de propositions, tant d'exclamations, de surprise bien
    contenue,
Et tant de secrets gardés et tant d'aveux sans formule,
Tout cela devenu poil et naseaux bien à leur place,
Et humidité de l'oeil.
Visages toujours sans précédent tant ils occupent l'air
    hardiment!
Qui dira les mots non sortis des vaches, des limaçons, des
    serpents,
Et les pronoms relatifs des petits, des grands éléphants.
Mais avez-vous besoin des mots, visages non bourdonnants,
Et n'est-ce pas le silence qui vous donne votre sereine
    profondeur,
Et ces espaces intérieurs qui font qu'il y a des vaches sacrées
    et des tigres sacrés.
Oh! je sais que vous aboyez, vous beuglez et vous mugissez
Mais vous gardez pour vous vos nuances et la source de votre
    espérance
Sans laquelle vous ne sauriez faire un seul pas, ni respirer.
Oreilles des chevaux, mes compagnons, oreilles en cornet
Vous que j'allais oublier,
Qui paraissez si bien faites pour recevoir nos confidences
Et les mener en lieu sûr,
Par votre chaud entonnoir qui bouge à droite et à gauche...
Pourquoi ne peut-on dire des vers à l'oreille de son cheval
Sans voir s'ouvrir devant soi les portes de l'hôpital.
Chevaux, quand ferez-vous un clin d'oeil de connivence
Ou un geste de la patte.
Mais quelle gêne, quelle envie de courir à toutes jambes cela
    produirait dans le monde

Visages of Animals

Visages of animals
So well moulded from inside because of all the words
    you haven't known how to say,
So many proposals, so many exclamations of well-contained
    surprise
And so many secrets kept and so many avowals without
    formula,
All of which became fur and nostrils properly in their place
And moisture of the eye.
Visages forever without precedent, so boldly do they occupy
    the air!
Who will speak the words not issued from cows, snails, and
    serpents
And the relative pronouns of the little and big elephants?
But do you need words, visages that don't hum,
For isn't it silence that gives you your serene depth
And those interior spaces that make possible sacred cows
    and sacred tigers?
Oh, I know that you bark, bellow and roar
But you keep to yourself your nuances and the source of
    your hope
Without which you wouldn't know how to take a single step
    or breath.
Ears of horses, my companions, trumpet ears,
You that I was going to forget,
That seem to be so well made to receive our confidences
And to lead them to a safe place
Through your warm funnel that moves from right to left...
Why can't one recite verses in the ear of his horse
Without seeing the doors of the asylum opening up before him?
Horses, when will you give us a wink of connivance
Or a gesture of the foreleg?
But what trouble, what a desire to run away full speed
    your winking and gesturing would produce in the world!

On ne serait plus jamais seul dans la campagne ni en forêt
Et dès qu'on sortirait de sa chambre
Il faudrait se cacher la tête sous une étoffe foncée.

One would never be alone in the countryside or in the forest
And from the moment a person walked out of his room
He would have to hide his head under a dark cloth.

Docilité

La forêt dit: "C'est toujours moi la sacrifiée,
On me harcèle, on me traverse, on me brise à coups de hache,
On me cherche noise, on me tourmente sans raison,
On me lance des oiseaux à la tête ou des fourmis dans les
    jambes,
Et l'on me grave des noms auxquels je ne puis m'attacher.
Ah! on ne le sait que trop que je ne puis me défendre
Comme un cheval qu'on agace ou la vache mécontente.
Et pourtant je fais toujours ce que l'on m'avait dit de faire,
On m'ordonna: "Prenez racine." Et je donnai de la racine tant
    que je pus,
"Faites de l'ombre." Et j'en fis autant qu'il était raisonnable,
"Cessez d'en donner l'hiver." Je perdis mes feuilles jusqu'à la
    dernière.
Mois par mois et jour par jour je sais bien ce que je dois faire.
Voilà longtemps qu'on n'a plus besoin de me commander.
Alors pourquoi ces bûcherons qui s'en viennent au pas cadencé?
Que l'on me dise ce qu'on attend de moi, et je le ferai,
Qu'on me réponde par un nuage ou quelque signe dans le ciel,
Je ne suis pas une révoltée, je ne cherche querelle à personne
Mais il me semble tout de même que l'on pourrait bien me
    répondre
Lorsque le vent qui se lève fait de moi une questionneuse."

Docility

The forest says, "I'm always the one who's sacrificed,
They harass me, they tramp all over me, they smash me
    with their axes,
They try to pick a quarrel with me, they torment me
    for no reason,
They fling birds at my head and ants at my legs
And they carve names in me for which I have no affection.
Ah, they know only too well that I can't defend myself
Like a horse that's provoked or a discontented cow,
Even though I always do what they tell me to do.
They ordered me, 'Take root!' And I gave as much root
    as I could.
'Make shade!' And I made as much of it was was reasonable.
'Stop making it in winter!' I dropped my leaves down to
    the last one.
Month by month and day by day I know perfectly well
    what I have to do,
But it's been a long time since they last needed to
    order me about.
Then why are these lumberjacks approaching in lockstep?
Let someone tell me what's expected of me and I'll do it.
Let someone answer me with a cloud or some sign in the sky.
I'm not a rebel, I'm not looking to argue with anyone.
But just the same it seems to me it would be nice if
    they answered me
When the rising wind makes a questioner of me."

La mer secrète

Quand nul ne la regarde,
La mer n'est plus la mer,
Elle est ce que nous sommes
Lorsque nul ne nous voit.
Elle a d'autres poissons,
D'autres vagues aussi.
C'est la mer pour la mer
Et pour ceux qui en rêvent
Comme je fais ici.

The Secret Sea

When no one looks at her
The sea is no longer the sea.
She is what we are
When no one looks at us.
Indeed, she has other fish
And other waves besides.
She is the sea for the sea
And for those who dream of her
As I do here.

Chevaux sans cavaliers

Il était une fois une cavalerie
Longuement dispersée
Et les chevaux trempaient leur cou dans l'avenir
Pour demeurer vivants et toujours avancer.

Et dans leur sauvagerie ils galopaient sans fatigue.

Tout noirs et salués d'alarmes au passage
Ils couraient à l'envi, ou tournaient sur eux-mêmes,
Ne s'arrêtant que pour mourir
Changer de pas dans la poussière et repartir.

Et des poulains fièvreux rattrapaient les juments.

Il est tant de chevaux qui passèrent ici
Ne laissant derrière eux qu'un souvenir de bruit.
Je veux vous écouter, galops antérieurs,
D'une oreille précise,
Que mon coeur ancien batte dans ma clairière
Et que, pour l'écouter, mon coeur de maintenant
Etouffe tous ses mouvements
Et connaisse une mort ivre d'être éphémère.

Horses Without Riders

Once upon a time there was a cavalry troop
Long disbanded
And the horses would drench their necks in the future
To stay alive and to move forever forward.

And in their wildness they would gallop tirelessly.

Utterly black and greeted with fright on the way
They would run as they pleased or spin round and round,
Stopping only to die,
Changing pace in the dust and setting off again.

And the feverish colts would catch up with the mares.

There are so many horses who passed by here,
Leaving behind them only a memory of sound.
I want to listen to you, bygone gallops,
With an accurate ear.
Let my former heart beat in my clearing
And in order to hear it, let my present heart
Suppress all its movements
And endure a death, drunk with the short life.

1939-1945
1946

1940

...Nous sommes très loin en nous-mêmes
Avec la France dans les bras,
Chacun se croit seul avec elle
Et pense qu'on ne le voit pas.

Chacun est plein de gaucherie
Devant un bien si précieux,
Est-ce donc elle, la patrie,
Ce corps à la face des cieux?

Chacun la tient à sa façon
Dans une étreinte sans mesure
Et se mire dans sa figure
Comme au miroir le plus profond.

1940

. . .We are a long way into ourselves
With France in our arms.
Each believes he is alone with her
And thinks that no one sees.

Each is full of awkwardness
Before a gift so precious.
Is it really she, our country,
This body, face to the sky?

Each holds her in his own way
In an embrace beyond measure
And sees himself in her face
As in the deepest mirror.

Paris

O Paris, ville ouverte
Ainsi qu'une blessure,
Que n'es-tu devenue
De la campagne verte.

Te voilà regardée
Par des yeux ennemis,
De nouvelles oreilles
Écoutent nos vieux bruits.

La Seine est surveillée
Comme du haut d'un puits
Et ses eaux jour et nuit
Coulent emprisonnées.

Tous les siècles français
Si bien pris dans la pierre
Vont-ils pas nous quitter
Dans leur grande colère?

L'ombre est lourde de têtes
D'un pays étranger.
Voulant rester secrète
Au milieu du danger

S'éteint quelque merveille
Qui préfère mourir
Pour ne pas nous trahir
En demeurant pareille.

Paris

Oh Paris, open city,
Open like a wound,
What hasn't become of you
In your green surround.

You, stared at
By enemy eyes
While new ears listen
To our ancient sounds.

Our Seine is guarded
As from the height of a pit,
Her waters flow jailed
Day and night.

All the French centuries
So well caught in stone,
Are they going to quit us
In their giant rage?

The darkness is heavy with heads
From an alien land.
Wishing to endure in secret
In the midst of terror

A wonder passes away
Which prefers to die
Rather than betray us
By remaining the same.

La nuit . . .

La nuit, quand je voudrais changer dans un sommeil
Qui ne veut pas de moi, me laissant tout pareil,
Avec mon grand corps las et sans voix pour se plaindre,
Ma cervelle allumée, et je ne puis l'éteindre,
Le mort que je serai bouge en moi sans façons
Et me dit: "Je commence à trouver le temps long,
Qu'est-ce qui peut encor te retenir sur terre,
Après notre défaite et la France en misère."
Ne voulant pas répondre à qui partout me suit
Et cherchant plus avant un monde où disparaître,
J'étouffe enfin en moi le plus triste de l'être
Et me sens devenir l'humble fils de la nuit.

Night

In the night when I would wish to shift from a sleep
That desires me no longer, leaving me all as I am,
With my great body weary and voiceless to moan,
My brain on fire and I helpless to put it out,
The dead man I shall become stirs quietly in me
Saying, "Time is beginning to drag for me,
What is it that can still keep you on earth
After our defeat and France in misery?"
Not wishing to answer him who tracks me everywhere
And giving up the search for a world to vanish in,
I stifle in me at last the saddest of selves
And sense myself becoming the humble son of night.

Le relais

Petite halte dans la nuit
Où le sommeil s'en va sans bruit
De mes paupières relevées.
Ce doit être ici le relais
Où l'âme change de chevaux
Pour les trois heures du matin.
Ce sont de gris chevaux de feutre,
Leurs naseaux ne frémissent pas
Et l'on n'entend jamais leur pas
Même sous l'écorce de l'être.
J'ai beau me trouver dans mes draps
Ils me tirent sur une route
Que je ne puis apercevoir
Et j'ai beau rester à l'écoute
Je n'entends que mon coeur qui bat
Et résume dans son langage
Où je perçois quelques faux-pas
Son courage et mon décourage.
J'avance d'un pas incertain
Dans un temps proche et très lointain
Sous les décombres du sommeil.
Je suis sur les bancs de l'école
Parmi des enfants, mes pareils,
Et voilà que l'on m'interroge.
—Que donc était si malheureux?
—La France coupée au milieu.
—Qui souffrait d'espérer encor
Quand l'honneur même semblait mort?
J'étais trop triste pour répondre
Et devenais larmes dans l'ombre
Puis je reprenais le chemin
Qui conduisait au lendemain,
Tiré par des chevaux sans gloire
Hors de l'enfance et de l'Histoire
Jusqu'à ce que parût enfin
Modeste, le petit matin.

The Post House

Little stop in the night
Where sleep noiselessly slips away
From my raised eyelids.
This must be the inn
Where the soul changes horses
At three in the morning.
Grey horses of felt,
Their nostrils without a quiver,
Their hoofbeats never heard
Even under the shell of self.
It's no use being in the bedsheets,
They pull me onto a road
I can't make out.
And no use keeping my ears open,
All I hear is my beating heart
Summing up in its own language,
In which I note some errors,
Its courage and my discouragement.
I move on with uncertain step
In a time near and very far
Under the rubble of sleep.
I'm on my bench in school
Among the children, my peers,
For this interrogation:
"Who is so wretched?"
"France cut in two."
"Who can bear to hope
When honor itself seems dead?"
I was too sad to answer
And became tearful in the dark.
Then I took to the road again
Leading to the future,
Drawn by horses ingloriously
Out of childhood and out of History
Into the finally appearing
Modest dawn.

Famille de ce monde

Et des milliers de bourgeons viennent voir ce qui se passe au
    monde
Car la curiosité de la Terre est infinie.
Et l'enfant naît et sa petite tête mal fermée encore
Se met à penser dans le plus grand secret parmi les grandes
    personnes tout occupées de lui.
Et il est tout nu sous la pression exigeante de la lumière du jour
Tournant de côté et d'autre ses yeux presque aveugles au sortir
    de la nuit maternelle,
Emplissant la chambre, comme il peut, de ce vagissement venu
    d'un autre monde.
Et bien que parachevé, il s'ouvre encore à la fragilité dans ses
    délicates fontanelles
Tout en fermant très fort ses petits poings comme un homme
    barbu qui se met en colère.
Et sa mère est une géante bien intentionnée qui se dresse dans
    l'ombre et l'assume dans ses bras,
Encore stupéfaite d'entendre cette chair séparée qui a
    maintenant une voix,
Comme un pêcher qui entendrait crier sa pêche,
Ou l'olivier, son olive.
Mais dans l'ombre un sein qui blanchit dessine son cercle
    auroral
Et des lèvres toutes neuves, à peine finies, et qui ont grande
    hâte de servir
Tâtonnent à sa rencontre
Jusqu'à ce qu'on entende un petit bruit de la gorge
    compréhensive
Quand le lait se met à passer de la mère à l'enfant.
Et la vie va son chemin qu'elle sait ininterrompu
Sous le tic tac de la pendule
Car le Temps imbibe jour et nuit de son humidité invisible
    tout ce que nous faisons sur terre.
Mais il ne faudrait pas oublier que le père est dans la pièce
Et sentant à l'instant même sa parfaite inutilité
Il trouve que c'est le moment de regarder par la fenêtre

Family of this World

And thousands of buds come to see what is happening
    in the world
Because the curiosity of the Earth is infinite.
And the child is born and his still partly closed little head
Begins to think in the greatest secrecy in the midst of the
    big persons completely occupied with him.
And he is totally naked under the exacting pressure of daylight,
Turning his nearly blind eyes from side to side as the maternal
    night draws to a close,
Filling the room as he can with the cry of the newborn come
    from another world.
And although perfected, he is still open to the fragility in his
    delicate fontanelles
While clenching his little fingers very tightly like a bearded man
    who falls into a rage.
And his mother is a well-intentioned giantess who stands up
    in the dark and takes him in her arms,
Still stupefied to hear this separated flesh which now has a voice,
Like a peach tree that would hear its peach cry
Or the olive tree its olive.
But in the darkness a whitening breast makes its auroral circle
    visible
And entirely new lips, barely finished and in a great hurry
    to be of use,
Feel their way to their joining
Until one hears a little noise of the understanding throat
When the milk begins to pass from the mother to the child.
And life goes along its own way knowing it will be uninterrupted
By the tick tock of the clock
Because day and night Time saturates everything we do on earth
    with its invisible moisture.
But one shouldn't forget that the father is also in the room
And feeling at this very instant his perfect uselessness
He finds that it's just the moment to look out the window

Cependant que la grandeur du monde poursuit sa route béante
    dans une profonde anesthésie,
Et la Terre tourne sans effort comme en pensant à autre chose,
Et la Grand Ourse et Bételgeuse
Montrent leur face inhumaine à la portière du train terrestre
Qui n'a pas l'air de bouger bien qu'il avance toujours,
Et l'univers bien huilé fait moins de bruit
Que les pieds nus de l'enfant qui frottent l'un contre l'autre,
Car l'enfant est encore là, collé au globe maternel.

                                    Montevideo, Mars 1944.

While the grandeur of the world pursues its wide-open road
    in a deep anaesthesia,
And the Earth turns effortlessly as though it was thinking
    of something else,
And the Great Bear and the Betelgeuse
Show their inhuman faces at the door of the terrestrial train
Which doesn't seem to be stirring even though it's always
    moving forward,
And the well-oiled universe makes less noise
Than the naked feet of the child who rubs them against
    each other
Because the child is still there, glued to the maternal globe.

                              Montevideo, March 1944

C'est la terre sans nous et les arbres sans nous,
Ma fenêtre sans moi pour écrire derrière d'une main de vivant,
C'est mon lit qui soutiendra un corps inconnu, de poids
    différent du mien,
Avec une tête tout autre et peut-être furieuse, qui sortira des
    couvertures,
C'est le ciel bleu quand mes yeux auront cessé d'être bleus,
Et que je ne serai plus une ruche visitée par la poésie.
C'est la mer qui sera encor la mer quand on m'aura changé
En l'ombre évasive d'un poisson dans l'eau de la mémoire
    glauque.
Et c'est le coeur de mes enfants qui continuera de battre
Lorsque je ne vivrai qu'en eux, fort maigrement à l'abri,
Car mon sang, ce vieil intrus, intimidé par leur sang jeune
Ne saura trop comment faire pour manifester sa présence
Attendant un moment plus favorable, et remettant au
    lendemain,
Puis tout d'un coup enhardi par son autorité clandestine
Il affleurera brusquement sur leur très jeune visage
Et voilà que mon enfant me ressemblera bien plus fort
Et en rougira de plaisir à moins que ce ne soit de colère.
O mes filles, l'on prétend que vous me ressemblez aussi,
Comment fites-vous pour loger ce grand diable de dyspeptique
Dans votre corps féminin si parfaitement ajusté,
Et comment avez-vous pu de mon nez fort téméraire,
Composer ce nez modeste qui tient la place qu'il faut
Dans un visage très pur...
Mais ce n'est tout encore.
Alors que l'on pensait en avoir fini avec moi
Voilà que je reparais, comme un chasseur à l'affût
Dans les yeux de vos enfants,
Et, complice d'un poupon, j'agite mes bras avec lui,
Le fais crier à tue-tête,

Without Us

It's the earth without us and the trees without us,
My window without me to write behind with the hand of a
    living person,
It's my bed supporting an unknown body with a weight
    different from mine,
With an altogether different head, perhaps furious, which will
    emerge from the covers,
It's the blue sky when my eyes will have ceased being blue,
And it's me, no longer a hive visited by poetry.
It's the sea which will still be the sea when I shall have changed
Into the evasive shadow of a fish in the dull blue-green water
    of memory.
And it's the hearts of my children which will continue to beat
When I'll be living only in them, most meagerly sheltered,
Because my blood, that old intruder, intimidated by their
    young blood
Won't know too well how to demonstrate its presence,
Awaiting a more favorable moment and putting things off
    until tomorrow,
Then suddenly emboldened by its clandestine authority
Will surface abruptly on their very young faces—
And that's how my child will resemble me so strongly
And will flush with pleasure from my blood, unless it be
    with anger.
Oh my daughters, people say that you resemble me, too,
What did you do to lodge this great devil of a dyspeptic
In your perfectly regulated female bodies
And how have you been able with my strongly reckless nose
To compose this modest nose which takes its necessary place
In a very pure face . . .
But that's not all.
When you thought you had finished with me
There I was back again like a hunter lying in wait
In the eyes of your children
And, accomplice of a baby, I wave my arms with him,
Making him cry at the top of his voice

Et nous emplissons la chambre de notre collaboration
Comme deux coqs mêlent leurs chants dans l'air matinal.
Qu'on se rassure! Cela se passera entre os et peau,
La conversation se poursuivra dans le plus grand naturel,
On ne se doutera même pas que dans la nuit de la chair,
Il est un témoin subreptice, un témoin juge et partie,
Tant bien que mal retenu
Par l'humble cordon de brouillard qui va des enfants aux aïeux.

And we fill the room with our collaboration
Like two roosters blending their crowing in the morning air.
Put your mind at ease! All of that will take place between
    bone and skin,
The conversation will continue most naturally.
It will not even be suspected that in the night of the flesh
There exists a surreptitious witness, a witness who is both
    judge and litigant,
Held back after a fashion
By the humble strand of mist which runs from the children
    to the forefathers.

Arbres dans la nuit et le jour

Candélabres de la noirceur,
Hauts-commissaires des ténèbres,
Malgré votre grandeur funèbre
Arbres, mes frères et mes soeurs,
Nous sommes de même famille,
L'étrangeté se pousse en nous
Jusqu'aux veinules, aux ramilles,
Et nous comble de bout en bout.

A vous la sève, à moi le sang,
A vous la force, à moi l'accent
Mais nuit et jour nous ressemblant,
Régis par le suc du mystère,
Offerts à la mort, au tonnerre,
Vivant grand et petitement,
L'infini qui nous désaltère
Nous fait un même firmament.

Nos racines sont souterraines,
Notre front dans le ciel se perd
Mais, tronc de bois ou coeur de chair,
Nous n'avançons que dans nous-mêmes.
L'angoisse nourrit notre histoire
Et c'est un même bûcheron
Qui, nous couchant de notre long,
Viendra nous couper la mémoire.

Enfants de la chance et du vent,
Vous n'avez de père ni mère,
Vous êtes fils d'une grand'mère
La Terre, son vieil ornement,
Vous qui devenez innombrables
Dans vos branches comme à vos pieds
Et pouver attraper du ciel
Aussi bien que fixer les sables.

Trees by Night and Day

Candelabra of blackness,
High commissioners of the dark,
Despite your funereal grandeur,
Trees, my brothers and sisters,
We're members of the same family.
The same strangeness moves in us
Down to the veinlets and the twigs
And fills us up from head to foot.

In you the sap, in me the blood,
In you force, in me intensity,
But night and day we're like each other,
Ruled by the ichor of mystery,
Offered up to death and thunder,
Living well and living meanly.
The infinite that quenches us
Creates our single firmament.

Our roots are underground,
Our brow is lost in the sky,
But trunk of wood or heart of flesh
We only progress into ourselves.
Agony nourishes our history
And the self-same woodcutter,
Seeing us lying outstretched,
Will come to cut our memory.

Children of chance and of wind
You have neither father nor mother.
You are offspring of a grandmother,
The Earth, her ancient ornament,
You who become innumerable
In your branches as in your feet
And can entrap the sky
As well as fasten sand.

Princes de l'immobilité,
Les oiseaux vous font confiance,
Vous savez garder le secret
D'un nid jusqu'à la délivrance.
A l'abri de vos coeurs touffus,
Vous façonnez toujours des ailes,
Et les projetez jusqu'aux nues
De votre arc secret mais fidèle.

Vous n'aurez pas connu l'amour,
O grandioses solitaires,
Toujours prisonniers de la Terre,
O Narcisses ligneux et sourds,
Ne regrettez pas l'aventure,
Heureux ceux que fixe le sort,
Ils en attendent mieux la mort,
Un voyageur vous en assure.

Princes of immobility,
The birds confide in you.
You know how to keep the secret
Of a nest until the hatching time.
In the shelter of your leafy hearts
You forever fashion wings
And sail them up to the clouds
Of your secret but exact arc.

You will not have known love,
Oh grandiose solitaries,
Forever prisoners of Earth.
Oh woody and deaf Narcissi,
Don't long for that adventure.
Happy are those whose fate is fixed,
They are better at awaiting death.
A voyager assures you so.

S'il n'etait pas d'arbres à ma fenêtre

S'il n'était pas d'arbres à ma fenêtre
Pour venir voir jusqu'au profond de moi,
Depuis longtemps il aurait cessé d'être
Ce coeur offert à ses brûlantes lois.

Dans ce long saule ou ce cyprès profond
Qui me connaît et me plaint d'être au monde,
Mon moi posthume est là qui me regarde
Comprenant mal pourquoi je tarde et tarde...

If There Were No Trees at My Window

If there were no trees at my window
To come and peer into the depths of me
This heart given over to its ardent laws
Would long ago have ceased to be.

In that long willow or dark cypress
That knows me and pities me being in the world,
Is my posthumous self who stares at me,
Comprehending poorly why I stay and stay...

A un arbre

Avec un peu de feuillage et de tronc
Tu dis si bien ce que je ne sais dire
Qu'à tout jamais je cesserais d'écrire
S'il me restait tant soit peu de raison.

Et tout ce que je voudrais ne pas taire
Pour ce qu'il a de perdu et d'obscur
Me semble peu digne que j'éclaire
Lorsque je mets une racine à nu

Dans son mutisme et ses larmes de terre.

To a Tree

With a bit of leaf and of trunk
You say so well what I don't know how to say
That I ought to quit writing forever
If I had any sense left in me.

And everything I'd like not to silence
Of whatever there is of lost and obscure
Seems to me less worth illuminating
After I strike a root naked

In its speechlessness and its tears of earth.

Tu disparais

Tu disparais, déjà te voilà plein de brume
Et l'on rame vers toi comme au travers du soir,
Tu restes seul parmi les ans qui te consument
Dans tes bras la minceur de tes derniers espoirs.

Où tu poses le pied viennent des feuilles mortes
Au souffle faiblissant d'anciennes amours,
La lune qui te suit prend tes dernières forces
Et te bleuit sans fin pour ton ultime jour.

Pourtant l'on voit percer sous ta candeur chagrine
Tout ce peu qui te reste et fait battre ton coeur
Et parfois un sursaut te hausse et t'illumine
Qui suscite en ta nuit des hiboux de splendeurs.

You are Disappearing

You are disappearing, already you stand there full of fog
And one rows towards you as across an evening.
You remain alone among the years that consume you,
In your arms the slenderness of your last hopes.

Wherever you place your foot dead leaves appear
With the weakening breath of bygone loves.
The moon which follows you absorbs the last of your strength
And tinges you an endless blue for your final day.

Yet one sees all the little that remains to you and makes your
       heart beat
Pierce your melancholy guilelessness
And sometimes a start lifts you and illuminates you
Arousing splendors in your night of owls.

Le mort en peine

Perdu parmi les pas et les ruines des astres
Et porté sur l'abîme où s'engouffre le ciel,
J'entends le souffle en moi des étoiles en marche
Au fond d'un coeur, hélas, que je sais éternel.
J'arrive de la Terre avec ma charge humaine
D'espoirs pris de panique et d'abrupts souvenirs,
Mais que faire en plein ciel d'un coeur qui se démène
Comme sous le soleil et n'as pas su mourir.
Avez-vous vu mes yeux errer dans ces parages
Où le loin et le près ignorent les rivages.
Aveugle sans bâton et sans force et sans foi,
Je cherche un corps, celui que j'avais autrefois.
Puissé-je préserver des avides espaces
Mes souvenirs rôdant autour de la maison,
Les visages chéris et ma pauvre raison
D'où je me surveillais comme d'une terrasse.
Que je sauve du moins ce vacillant trésor
Comme un chien aux longs poils sous l'écume marine
Qui tient entre ses dents son petit presque mort.
Mais voici s'avancer l'écume des abîmes...
L'univers où je suis pousse un cruel soupir
Et la gorge du ciel profonde se soulève.
Puisque tout me rejette ici, même le rêve,
Ces lieux sans terre, à quoi pourraient-ils consentir?

*

Ah! même dans la mort je souffre d'insomnies,
Je veux de l'éternel faire un peu de présent,
Je me sens encore vert pour entrer au néant
Et chante mal dans l'universelle harmonie.
Comment renoncerais-je à tant de souvenirs
Quand l'esprit encombré d'invisibles bagages
Je suis plus affairé dans la mort qu'en voyage
Et je flotte au lieu de sombrer dans le mourir.

The Dead Man Grieves

Lost among the footsteps and ruins of stars
And drawn into the abyss that devours the sky
I hear the breathing in me of stars on the march
In the depths of a heart, alas, I know to be eternal.
I come from Earth with all my human freight
Of panic-stricken hopes and abrupt memories—
But what does one do in the open sky with a heart that
    thrashes about
As if still under the sun, not knowing how to die?
Have you seen my eyes wandering in these parts
Where the far and the near are ignorant of shores?
Blind without a cane and without strength or faith
I'm looking for a body, the one I once had.
May I defend from avid space
All the memories roaming around my house,
All the dear faces and my poor reason
From which I overlooked myself as from a terrace.
Let me at least save this vacillating treasure
Like a long-haired dog in the sea-foam
Gripping his nearly dead little one with his teeth.
But here comes the foam of the abyss...
The universe around me heaves a cruel sigh
And the deep gorge of the sky rises.
Since everything rejects me here, even dream itself,
What can I hope for from these landless places?

*

Ah, even in death I suffer from insomnia,
I want to make a bit of the present out of the eternal,
I'm still too spry to enter the void
And I sing off-key in the universal harmony.
How can I renounce so many memories
When, with my mind encumbered by invisible baggage,
I'm busier dead than when I traveled
And I float on death instead of sinking down in.

Les quatre bouts de bois qui me tenaient sous terre
N'empêchaient pas le ciel d'entrer au cimetière,
Le monde me devient un immense radeau
Où l'âme va et vient sans trouver son niveau,
Tout se relève avec la pierre de la tombe,
Notre premier regard délivre cent colombes.
Pour qui ne possédait que sa longueur de bois,
Les arbres, c'est déjà le plus bel au-delà.

The four planks of wood which kept me underground
Never prevented the sky from entering the cemetery.
The world becomes an immense raft for me
On which my soul comes and goes without finding its balance.
Everything rises again as the stone of the tomb rises.
Our first glance frees a hundred doves.
For him possessing only his own length in wood
Trees are still the loveliest hereafter.

Oublieuse Mémoire
1948

Naissance de Venus

Les Heures

Voyez l'onde qui se teint de rouge, comme elle bouillonne!
C'est le sang d'Uranus qui tomba du haut ciel.
Comme dans l'eau le fer rouge, il fait un long bruissement.
Regardez, sans tenir compte des lentes coulées humaines
Une vierge nait soudain de la vague fécondée.
Déesse, elle est la déesse écumeuse et dans ses yeux
A distance de caresse
Sont les grandes profondeurs
Qui se dérobaient à nous au secret de l'océan.

Vénus

Je sors du marin murmure avec paroles à la bouche,
Je nais fille déjà grande
Et je vous regarde en face,
Ruisselante de beaux jours
Que je n'aurai pas vécus.
Je suis là de plus en plus
Comme un coeur touché d'amour
Et mon corps est plein de lignes,
Filles de mon harmonie.

Le Vent

Naviguant sur votre conque, laissez le jeune homme Vent
Vous pousser vers le rivage où vous appellent les Heures.
Née de la mer, c'est sur terre
Que vous attend l'avenir
Et précieuse comme l'air
Rien en vous ne peut finir.

Birth of Venus

The Hours

See the wave dyeing itself red, how it bubbles up!
It's the blood of Uranus who fell from high heaven.
Like a red-hot iron in the water, it makes a long seething.
Look, without bearing in mind the slow human flows,
A virgin is suddenly born from the fertile wave.
Goddess, she is the foamy goddess and in her eyes,
The distance of a caress,
Are the great depths
That steal away from us to the secret of the ocean.

Venus

I come out of the murmuring marine with words in my mouth.
I am born as a full-grown young woman
And I look you in the face
Streaming with lovely days
That I shall not have lived.
I am there more and more
Like a heart touched with love
And my body is full of curves,
Daughters of my harmony.

The Wind

Sailing on your conch, let the young man Wind
Push you towards the shore where the Hours are calling you.
Born of the sea, it is on earth
That the future awaits you
And precious as the air
Nothing in you can end.

Les Heures

Voici la Terre et ses arbres,
Voice la Terre et ses hommes
Et leurs têtes bourdonnantes
Comme le haut des forêts.
Approchez, voici venir d'insolites messagers,
Et pour mieux vous adorer
Le passereau se fait cygne et le cygne devient ange
Et la colombe, colombe!

The Hours

This is the Earth and its trees,
This is the Earth and its men
And their heads humming
Like the heights of the forests.
Come closer, here come strange messengers
And to better adore you
The sparrow makes himself swan and the swan becomes angel
And the dove, dove!

Champs-Élysées

Savez-vous que chaque jour cent poètes d'Amérique,
Remontent sans être vus l'Avenue des Champs-Élysées,
Et cent autres la descendent,
Et pendant le défilé, les marronniers cèdent la place à des
    palmiers hauts sur pied,
Savez-vous que leur ferveur s'allume phosphorescente,
Et toute circulation en serait interrompue
Si les poètes n'arrangeaient les choses, avec le tact des fantômes,
A mesure qu'ils les dérangent.
Familiers de l'impossible et sur le bord du désordre,
Ils remettent tout en place,
Les passants les plus futés ne s'aperçoivent de rien.
Mais quel est donc ce bruit sourd sur les côtes d'Amérique?
Ce sont les poètes de France qui débarquent là-bas leurs doubles.
Ohé Pablo et Alfonso, Jorge Luis, Carlos, Roberto, ohé Mario
    et Manuel et Augusto Frederico,
Ohé Sara et Gabriela, ohé Silvina et Juana, ohé Orfila
    et Cecilia
Voici les amis de France!
Interpellons-nous à voix forte à cause de ces espaces
    qui voudraient se mettre entre nous,
Même dans sa chambre, un poète est entouré de ses forêts,
Ouvertes, les portes, les fenêtres pour laisser passer la nature.
O poètes, rapprochons nos chaises à travers tout l'océan,
Elles n'en seront pas troublées ni le moins du monde mouillées,
Etant chaises de poètes,
Et s'il en est de boiteuses, c'est que la Terre a souffert.
Cinq ans durant, les étoiles ne brillèrent sur la France
    que jumelées à l'étoile innombrable de la mort,
Et l'aube, combien de fois armée comme une ennemie,
O poètes de la France, vous précéda clandestine
Pour se retourner tout d'un coup et vous fusiller le coeur.
Poètes des deux rivages,

Champs Élysées

Do you know that every day one hundred poets from the
    Americas
Go up the Avenue des Champs-Élysées without being seen
And a hundred others go down it
And during the procession the chestnut trees turn the place
    over to palm trees standing tall?
Do you know that their fervor lights up phosphorescently
And all traffic would be interrupted
If the poets didn't arrange things with the tact of phantoms
In proportion as they disturbed them?
Familiars of the impossible and on the edge of disorder
They put everything back again
So that the sharpest passersby notice nothing.
But what is that muffled noise on the coasts of America?
It's the poets of France who are disembarking their doubles
    over there.
Ohé Pablo and Alfonso, Jorge Luis, Carlos, Roberto,
    ohé Mario and Manuel and Augusto Frederico,
Ohé Sara and Gabriela, ohé Silvina and Juana, ohé Orfila and
    Cecilia
Here are your friends from France!
Let's call out loudly because of those distances which would
    like to place themselves between us,
Even in his room a poet is surrounded by his forests—
Open the doors and windows and let nature pass!
Oh poets, let's bring our chairs together across the ocean!
Getting wet won't trouble them the least bit,
Being chairs of poets—
And if some of them are wobbly it's because the Earth has
    suffered.
For five years the stars only shone on France coupled to the
    unnumbered star of death—
And the dawn, how many times armed like an enemy,
Preceded you secretly, Oh poets of France,
In order to wheel suddenly and shoot you in the heart.
Poets of the two shores,

Nous qui buvons nuit et jour à la fraîche source du monde
Et qui sommes familiers du pur compas des étoiles,
Traçons ensemble un arc-en-ciel avec ses couleurs scrupuleuses
(Nous laissons aux militaires leurs arcs de triomphe de pierre),
Notre grand pont suspendu chuchotera dans les airs,
Il veillera sur la terre,
Il brillera même la nuit sans effaroucher les astres,
Et penchons-nous sur la paix qui a le teint un peu jaune.
Que son sourire fragile prenne force en notre chant!
Il est temps que les hommes fassent comme s'ils étaient
     sans armes,
Même pas, au fond de leurs poches, un petit canif innocent!

April 1946.

We who drink night and day at the fresh spring of the world
And who are familiars of the pure compass of the stars,
Let's trace together the arch of a rainbow with its scrupulous
    colors
(We leave to the military their triumphal arches of stone).
Our great suspension bridge will whisper in the skies,
It will watch over the earth,
It will even shine at night without scaring the stars.
And let's lean towards the peace, whose complexion is a trifle
    yellow.
May its fragile smile draw strength from our song!
It's time that men act as if they were without weapons,
Not even, at the bottom of their pockets, a little innocent
    penknife!

April 1946

La mer

C'est tout ce que nous aurions voulu faire et n'avons pas fait,
Ce qui a voulu prendre la parole et n'a pas trouvé les mots
    qu'il fallait,
Tout ce qui nous a quittés sans rien nous dire de son secret,
Ce que nous pouvons toucher et même creuser par le fer
    sans jamais l'atteindre,
Ce qui est devenu vagues et encore vagues parce qu'il se cherche
    sans se trouver,
Ce qui est devenu écume pour ne pas mourir tout à fait,
Ce qui est devenu sillage de quelques secondes par goût
    fondamental de l'éternel,
Ce qui avance dans les profondeurs et ne montera jamais
    à la surface,
Ce qui avance à la surface et redoute les profondeurs,
Tout cela et bien plus encore,
La mer.

Cette mer qui a tant de choses à dire et les méprise,
Elle se veut toujours informulée,
Ou simplement murmurante,
Comme un homme qui bourdonne tout seul derrière ses dents,
    serrées,
Cette mer dont la surface est offerte au navire qui la parcourt,
Elle refuse ses profondeurs!
Est-ce pour contempler en secret sa nudité verticale
Qu'elle présente l'autre, à la lumière du ciel?
Et le ciel, au-dessus, offre sa grande coupe renversée
Pour faire comprendre à la mer qu'elle n'est pas faite
    pour la remplir,
Coupe et liquide demeurant ainsi face à face,
Collés l'un sur l'autre depuis les origines du monde,
Dans une vigilance sans fin qui ne tourne pas à leur confusion.
Et cependant,
Il est des yeux par paires qui regardent à bord du navire,
Mais ils ne voient guère mieux que des yeux d'aveugle
    qui vont aussi par paires.

The Sea

It's all that we would have wanted to do and haven't done,
That which has wanted to begin speaking and hasn't found
    the necessary words,
All that which has abandoned us without telling us anything
    of its secret,
That which we can touch and even plough with iron without
    ever attaining,
That which has become waves and waves again because it
    looks for itself without finding itself,
That which has become foam in order not to wholly die,
That which has become the wake of a few seconds because
    of a fundamental taste for the eternal,
That which moves into the depths and will never climb to
    the surface,
That which moves to the surface and dreads the depths,
All that and still much more,
The sea.

This sea which has so many things to say and despises them,
Who wishes herself to be always unformulated,
Or simply murmuring,
Like someone who hums all alone behind clenched teeth—
This sea whose surface is offered to the ship which travels her,
Refuses her depths!
Is it in order to contemplate in secret her vertical nakedness
That she presents the other to the light of the sky?
And the sky above offers its great upside-down cup
To make the sea understand that she is not made to fill it,
Cup and liquid remaining thus face to face,
Pressed against each other since the origins of the world
In an endless vigilance which doesn't become confusion.
And nevertheless,
There are eyes in pairs which are gazing from shipboard,
But they hardly see better than blind eyes which also go in pairs.

Devant la mer sous mes yeux je ne parviens à rien saisir,
Je suis devant un beau jour et ne sais plus m'en servir.
Trop d'océan, trop de ciel
En long, en large, en travers,
Je deviens un peu d'écume qui s'éteint et qui s'allume
Et change de position sur la couche de la mer.
Je ne sais plus où je suis, je ne sais plus où j'en suis.
Nous disions donc que ce jour,
Ce jour ne laissera pas de traces dans ma mémoire.

Confronting the sea below me I can reach nothing to seize,
I'm faced with a beautiful day and I no longer know how to
    use it.
Too much ocean, too much sky
In length, in width and crosswise.
I become a bit of foam which extinguishes itself and lights up
And changes position on the bed of the sea.
I no longer know where I am, I no longer know where I belong.
We were saying then that this day,
This day will leave no traces in my memory.

Premiers jours du monde

(Dieu Parle)

Je me dépêche avec le lièvre,
Je me mouille avec le poisson,
Je me cache avec la belette,
Je m'envole avec le pigeon,
Je m'endors avec l'homme heureux,
Je le réveille de bonne heure,
Je me cherche avec le boiteux,
J'éclate avec l'enfant qui pleure.
Et j'épouse de ma lumière
Tout ce qui bouge sur la terre
Et tout ce qui ne bouge plus.
Et je veux que tout signifie
Qu'à son Dieu toujours l'on se fie.
La chèvre sur le roc pointu,
Les pétales de la lumière,
Les nuages discontinus
Comme les montagnes altières
Allient leurs mots avec tant d'art
Qu'ils forment des phrases entières,
Et s'ils se taisent pour l'oreille,
Ils s'enchaînent pour le regard.
Langage à toutes les distances,
Creusé, bombé par les couleurs
Et dont la sereine éloquence
Toujours se déroule sans heurts
Dans le grand silence apparent,
Où tous parlent en même temps.

First Days of the World

(God Speaks)

I hurry with the hare,
I'm drenched with the fish,
I hide with the weasel,
I fly off with the pigeon,
I doze with the happy man,
I wake him early,
I'm one with the lame man,
I cry out with the child who cries
And I marry with my light
All who move on earth
And all who move no more.
And I wish everything to signify
That one always trusts his God.
The goat on the pointed rock,
The petals of light,
The intermittent clouds
Like mountains aloft
Combine their words with such art
That they form entire phrases
And if they are silent for the ear
They are linked for the eye—
Language leaping every distance,
Scooped or swollen by color,
And whose serene eloquence
Always smoothly unrolls
In the great seeming silence
Where all speak at once.

L'ennemi prenait tous les masques et se déguisait en n'importe
   quoi,
La belle journée, la moisson, le bouquet de roses
Devenaient soudain fous furieux et vous mordaient à mort
   dans une explosion,
Et l'on mourait tellement que la multitude se faisait de plus
   en plus souterraine.
Villes et villages savaient qu'ils pouvaient devenir cadavres
Avec autant d'empressement qu'un vivant peut faire un mort.
Les églises que la main rugueuse des siècles avait tant de fois
   caressées
Tombaient à terre tout d'un coup, frappées d'une attaque
   d'épilepsie, une seule, dont elles ne se relevaient qu'en
   poussière à tous les vents,
Et des chênes plusieurs fois centenaires traversaient l'air
   tout d'un coup comme des hirondelles en fuite.
La guerre changeait les joyaux les plus précieux en poudre
   sèche qui faisait tousser et cracher le sang.
Tout ce qui avait un corps sous le ciel se sentait devenir
   brouillard
Et chacun avait à la bouche le goût de ses propres cendres.
Mais un jour les hommes se chuchotèrent à l'oreille: "C'est
   la paix."
Et cela parut si étrange qu'ils ne reconnaissaient plus le son
   de leur voix,
Puis le murmure s'élargit qui répétait: "C'est la paix" et cela
   battait l'air gauchement comme un claquement d'ailes
   de pigeons
Et sous tant de souffrance étagée le mot "victoire" avait
   disparu du vocabulaire des hommes,
Et peu à peu toute la terre encore fraîchement retournée
   par la mort et les blessés se mit à chanter: "C'est la paix"
   de son gosier enroué.
La charrette retrouve ses roues et le cheval ses pattes de
   devant et de derrière pour galoper,

War and Peace on Earth

The enemy took all the masks and disguised himself as no
    matter what.
The lovely day, the harvest, the bouquet of roses
Suddenly went raving mad and bit you to death in an explosion
And a person died in such a way that the multitude became
    more and more subterranean.
Towns and villages knew that they were able to become
    cadavers
With as much willingness as a living person is able to become
    a dead one.
The churches which the rough hand of the centuries had so
    many times caressed
Fell to the ground suddenly, stricken with an attack of
    epilepsy, just one, from which they recovered only in
    dust to the four winds.
And the oaks, centenarians many times over, ascended the air
    suddenly like swallows in flight.
The war changed the most precious jewels into dry powder
    causing people to cough and spit blood.
Everyone who had a body under the sky felt himself becoming
    fog
And each one had in his mouth the taste of his own ashes.
But one day men whispered to each other,
"It's peace."
And that seemed so strange that they no longer recognized the
    sound of their own voices.
Then the murmur spread and repeated, "It's peace," and it
    beat the air awkwardly like a flapping of the wings of
    doves.
And under so many layers of suffering the word, "victory,"
    had disappeared from the vocabulary of men
And little by little the whole earth, still freshly turned up by
    death and the wounded, began to sing, "It's peace," with
    her hoarse throat.
The cart finds its wheels again and the horse his forelegs and
    hindlegs to gallop with,

Les arbres retrouvent leurs racines, dans la profondeur
enfoncées et leur sève n'est plus terrorisée, elle reprend
son cours jusqu'aux extrêmes ramilles.
L'église s'assure de son clocher jusqu'à sa pointe et ses
assises cessent de discuter leurs chances de vivre,
dans les soubassements.
Les moutons de la prairie rentrent dans leur laine et leur
profonde stupidité comme aux temps immémoriaux,
Et la vache redonne un lait couleur de la paix revenue,
La vie rentre de nouveau dans l'homme comme l'épée
au fourreau,
Le sang ne cherche plus le sang droit devant lui, dans le
ventre du prochain,
La face de l'ennemi ne luit plus toute proche comme un
instrument de torture doué de l'usage de la parole
Et la cantate "C'est la paix" fait lentement le tour de la terre
Et les morts à la guerre pour ne pas arriver en retard à
l'humble fête générale,
Descendent quatre à quatre leurs interminables escaliers
Et ils n'en finissent plus de descendre en courant dans le plus
grand tumulte silencieux,
Eux tous frustrés de leur vie, gesticulant et bougonnant,
réquisitionnent en nous une place en toute hâte
Pour voir, avec des yeux qui voient encore,
Le visage des vivants lorsque la paix est enfin revenue
sur la terre.

The trees find their roots again thrust into the depths and their
sap is no longer terrorized—it resumes its flow out to the
farthest twigs.
The church checks its steeple right up to the tip and its
foundations cease to discuss their chances of living in the
bedrock.
The meadow sheep retire into their wool and their profound
stupidity as in times immemorial
And the cow gives milk again the color of the new peace.
Life goes back into men like the sword into the sheath.
The blood no longer looks for the blood right in front of it in
the belly of its neighbor,
The face of the enemy no longer gleams close up like an
instrument of torture endowed with the use of speech
And the cantata, "It's peace," slowly circles the earth,
And the war dead in order not to arrive late at the humble
general holiday
Race down their interminable stairs
And never finish descending in their great silent tumult.
All those frustrated with their lives, gesticulating and
grumbling, commandeer a place among us as quickly as
possible
So they can see, with eyes that can still see,
The faces of the living when peace at last has come back to
the earth.

Naissances
1951

Le malade

Trop grand le ciel trop grand je ne sais où me mettre
Trop profond l'océan point de place pour moi
Trop confuse la ville trop claire la campagne.
Je fais ciel, je fais eau, sable de toutes parts,
Ne suis-je pas encore accoutumé a vivre
Suis-je un enfant boudeur qui ne veut plus jouer,
Oublié-je que si je tousse
Mes soixante-six ans tousseront avec moi
Et feront avec moi tousser mon univers.
Quand le matin je me réveille
Est-ce que je ne sors pas peu à peu tout entier
De l'an quatre-vingt-quatre, du siècle précédent
Où se font les vieillards?
Mais qui ose parler de vieillards alors que
Les mots le plus retors désarment sous ma plume,
Même le mot vieillard redoutable entre tous
Fait pivoter vers moi un tout neuf tournesol
Brillant comme un jeune homme.
Hache du désespoir taciturne en ma main
Tu te mets à chanter comme fait l'espérance.

The Sick Man

Too big the sky too big I don't know where to go
Too deep the sea no place for me
Too confused the town too serene the country.
I am sky, I am water, sand on all sides,
Haven't I grown used to living yet,
Am I a sulking child who doesn't want to play,
Am I forgetting that if I cough
My sixty six years will cough with me
And will make my world cough with me, too?
When I wake up in the morning
Doesn't my entire being gradually walk out
Of the year '84 of the last century
When old men are created?
But who dares speak of old men when
The craftiest words disarm beneath my pen.
Even the words old man, most fearsome of all,
Make a new sunflower, blooming
Like a young man, pivot toward me.
Hatchet of silent despair in my hand
You begin to sing as hope does.

Le Corps Tragique
1959

Finale

Cette bombe avait détruit
Même les anges du ciel
Et sans faire d'autre bruit
Qu'abeille faisant son miel.

Même les démons sous cape
Ou de méchants capuchons
Sans que rien ne les rattrape
Périssent sous son action.

Mais un seul agneau sans mère
Survécut à tout cela,
Au nom de toute la terre
Il bêla et s'en alla.

Finale

This bomb had destroyed
Even the angels in heaven,
Making no more noise
Than the bee making honey.

Even the demons under cloaks
Or evil hoods, without which
They can never be seized,
Perished in its action.

But a single motherless lamb
Survived all that.
In the name of all the earth
It bleated and died.

Reflections on the Art of Poetry 1951

Poetry comes to me from an always latent dream. I like to direct this dream except on days of inspiration when I have the impression that it directs itself.

I don't like the dream which just drifts (I was going to say which just dreams). I try to make a substantial dream of it, a kind of ship's figurehead which after crossing inner space and time confronts outside space and time—and for it the outside is the blank page.

To dream is to forget the materiality of one's body, to confuse in a way the outer and the inner world. The omnipresence of the cosmic poet has perhaps no other origin. I always dream a little that what I see, even at the precise moment of seeing and as I go along seeing, is what I experienced in *Boire à la Source*[1] and is always true; when I'm in the countryside the landscape suddenly becomes almost interior by I don't know what process of gliding from the outside to the inside and I move on in my own mental world.

People are sometimes surprised over my marvelling at the world; this occurs as much from the permanence of my dreams as from my bad memory. Both lead me from surprise to surprise and force me to be astonished at everything. "Why, there are trees, there is the sea. There are women. There are even very beautiful women..."

But if I dream I am not less drawn to poetry by a great precision in the dream, by a kind of hallucinated exactness. Isn't it in just that way that the dream manifests itself to the dreamer? It is perfectly defined even in its ambiguities. It is on waking that the shapes erase themselves and the dream becomes blurred, inconsistent.

If I have revealed myself fairly late in life it is because for a long time I eluded my deep self. I did not dare confront it directly and "Poèmes de l'Humour Triste"[2] resulted. I needed to have very strong nerves to face the vertigoes, the traps of the inner cosmos for which I have always had the most vivid and most co-enesthetic feelings.

I was long in coming to modern poetry, in being attracted to Rimbaud and Apollinaire. I couldn't leap the walls of flame and smoke which separate these poets from the classics and romantics. And if I may make a confession, one which is only a wish perhaps, I have attempted consequently to be one of those who dispersed that smoke in striving not to extinguish the flame, a conciliator, a reconciler of ancient and modern poetry.

Since poetry had been quite dehumanized, I proposed, in the continuity and light dear to the classics, to reveal the torments, hopes and anguish of a poet and a man of these times. I think of a certain virtually unknown preface of Valéry to a young poet. "Don't be dissatisfied with your verses," said the poet of *Charmes* to André Caselli. "I find exquisite qualities in them, of which one is essential for my taste; I'm speaking of a sincerity of tone which for the poet is the analogue of true pitch in singers. Keep this *real* tone. Don't be surprised that it's I who notice it in your poems and praise it. But the immense difficulty lies in combining this exact sound of the soul with the artifice of art. There must be enormous art in order to really be oneself and simple. But art alone would not know how to be enough."

This real and sincere tone, this simplicity, is what I, too, have always tried to retain; they were sufficiently submerged in my dreams not to stand in the way of poetry. People in our time have made such a goal of madness in verse and prose that this madness no longer has an appetizing virtue for me. I really find more spice and even mustard in a certain wisdom governing this madness and giving it the appearance of reason than in delirium abandoned to itself.

There is certainly an element of delirium in all poetic creation, but this delirium should be decanted and separated from the ineffective or harmful residue with all the precautions due such a delicate operation. For me it is only by dint of simplicity and transparency that I succeed in arriving at my essential secrets and in decanting my deepest poetry. I strain until the supernatural becomes natural and flows naturally (or seems to). I see to it that the ineffable becomes familiar at the same time that it guards its fabulous origins.

The poet has two pedals at his disposal, one clear permitting him to attain transparency, the other obscure ending in opaqueness. I think that I have only rarely pressed on the obscure pedal. If I veil I do so naturally and it is, I hope, only the veil of poetry. The poet often operates warmly in darkness, but the cold operation also has its advantages. It permits us greater audacities because they are more lucid. We know that we shall not blush over them one day as from a passing intoxication and transport we no longer understand. I need this lucidity all the more because I am naturally obscure. There is no poetry for me that doesn't begin with a certain confusion. I try to bring some light to it without making it lose its subconscious vitality.

I like the strange only when it is acclimated, brought to human temperature. I try my skill at making a straight line out of one or several broken lines. Some poets are often victims of their trances. They abandon themselves to the sole pleasure of their freedom and never worry about the beauty of the poem. Or to use another image, they fill their glass to the brim and forget to serve you, the reader.

I have scarcely known the fear of banality which haunts most writers, but fear rather to be thought incomprehensible and peculiar. Not writing for mystery specialists I have always suffered when a sensitive person has not understood one of my poems.

The image is the magic lantern which lights up the poets in the darkness. It is also the illuminated surface as the poet approaches that mysterious center where the very heart of poetry beats. But images are not all. There are passages from one image to the other which must also be poetry. As for analysis of poetry, people have said that it is anti-poetic and this is true if it is an analysis understood only by logicians. But there are things submerged in dream which can reveal themselves without leaving the realm of poetry.

Thus the poet can aspire to coherence, to the plausibility of the whole poem whose surface can be limpid while mystery takes refuge in the depths. I count on my poem to direct the images and make them sing true. As the poem bathes in me in an inner dream I'm not afraid to make it sometimes take the form of a narrative. The logic of the storyteller superintends the rambling reverie of the poet. The cohesion of the whole poem, far from destroying its magic, consolidates its foundations. And when I say that the storyteller superintends the poet in me I'm not losing sight, of course, of the differences among the literary genres. The story goes directly from one point to the other while the poem, as I generally conceive of it, advances in concentric circles.

I come from a family of small watchmakers who have worked all their lives with a magnifying glass screwed to their eyes. Therefore the least little springs must be in place if one wants the whole poem to set itself in motion under our eyes.

I don't wait for inspiration to write and I go out to meet it more than halfway along the road. The poet cannot count on the very rare moments when he writes as though under dictation. And it seems to me that he should imitate the man of science who doesn't wait for inspiration to start working. Science is an excellent school of modesty, if not the opposite, since it has confidence in the constant value of man and not only at some privileged moments. How often we think we have nothing to say while a poem is waiting in us behind a thin curtain of mist and it is enough to silence the noise of everyday life for the poem to unveil itself to us.

Stendhal had faith only in persistence in the writer. I think he was also thinking of the involuntary persistence which is the fruit of a long obsession. Sometimes what people call inspiration comes from the poet's benefitting from an unconscious and ancient persistence which ends up bearing fruit. It permits us to see in ourselves as though through a skylight that which is invisible at ordinary times.

I don't like a too eccentric originality (apart from some shining exceptions such as Lautréamont or Michaux in France). I prefer a less self-conscious originality as in our classics.

Despite the marvelous examples of some poets who transform words into precious objects, I often write without thinking of the words; I even strive to forget their existence in order to more and more tightly enclose my thought or rather that intermediate state between thought and dream that gives birth to the poem. It's not actually a question, properly speaking, of thinking in poetry but in some way giving its equivalent or nostalgia for it. I have tried to convey the feeling of creation, at least as I have experienced it, in the following passage, replying to an inquiry by Jean Paulham in the *Nouvelle Revue Française*. (But it is a state of lyrical intoxication which I have rarely felt in its fullness, and one can see in the preceding pages that I do not wait for a state of trance in order to write.) "Inspiration generally manifests itself in me by the feeling that I am everywhere at once, in space as well as in the diverse regions of the heart and mind. The state of poetry comes to me, therefore, from a kind of magical confusion where the ideas and images begin to live and abandon their lines of intersection, either to make advances to other images—in this nearby domain nothing is really distant—or to undergo profound metamorphoses which render them unrecognizable. However, for the mind confused with dreams opposites no longer exist; affirmation and negation become the same thing as do past and future, despair and hope, death and life. The inner song rises, it chooses the words that suit it. I give myself the illusion of assisting obscurity in its effort toward light while the moving images rise to the surface of the paper, calling out in the depths. After that I know a little better where I am with myself; I have created dangerous forces and I have exorcised them; I have made out of them allies of my innermost reason."

Paulhan told me that my statement was really a prose poem. This is because most of the time I move forward in my thought only by means of images. If the image, even when it is precise, is more imprecise than the concept, it radiates more and goes farther into the unconscious. It is embodied in the poem whereas the concept, more or less formulated, is there only for intelligibility and to permit the poem to attain another image which emerges little by little from the depths.

If there is some humanity in my poetry it is perhaps because I cultivate my poor soil with a well-tested fertilizer, suffering. And it is perhaps this dull continual anxiety which often prevents my poetry from being more brilliant. To suffer in one's body or in one's ideas is to think of oneself, to turn against oneself. To think of oneself, in spite of oneself, is to be impoverished and destitute of ornament. I have always more or less dreaded attacking the monsters I sense in me. I prefer to tame them with everyday words, which are the most reassuring of all. (Aren't they the very ones which quieted us during our great childish terrors?) I count on their wisdom and their friendship, tested many a time, to neutralize the venom of the strange, often the forerunner of panic. And perhaps I owe the best of my wisdom to the fact that I have often had to subdue a bit of madness.

I don't like in poetry (in mine, at least) a very apparent richness. I prefer richness to be muted and somewhat dimmed in its luster, if it has any. If it must reproduce itself let the miracle move forward stealthily and withdraw the same way after having done its deed. I like to force to the point of denuding them the most entangled sentiments and the strangest sensations that crowd within us. I also believe a great deal in the virtue of having some phrases in prose at the heart of a poem. (But they must be well accented and lifted by the rhythm.) By their great naturalness at a tragic moment they can bring an extraordinary pathos to the poem. When Victor Hugo hears "les noirs chevaux de la mort"[3] coming he adds these two lines which are pure prose (but divinely accented and rhythmed):

> "Je suis comme celui qui s'étant trop haté
> Attend sur le chemin que la voiture passe."[4]

I use many different poetic forms: regular verse (or almost), blank verse that rhymes when it comes to me, free verse, versicles that approach a rhythmic prose. Loving above all the natural I never say to myself beforehand that I shall use this or that form. I let my poem itself make the choice. This is not scorn but suppleness of technique. Or, if you prefer, an adaptable technique that fixes on each poem whose song it marries. A technique which permits a great variety of inspiration.

Poetic art is for each poet the more or less indiscreet praise of the poetry in which he excels. Thus Verlaine recommends to us "vers impairs,"[5] Valéry regular verse in a classic and Mallarméan form, Claudel the versicle. You must excuse me if I have stated my preferences with much more naiveté than my illustrious predecessors and with a nonchalance which is paired with reverie. I like to write without too much self-consciousness and preferably in a garden where nature seems to be doing all the work. Certainly the open air and spaces without walls impede concentration somewhat, but if the garden is enclosed they favor a directed distraction, friend of poetry, shade and freshness.

Each poet has his secrets. I have tried to tell you some of mine by unveiling this double of ourselves who watches us in the dark, approves us or makes us tear up the paper on which we have just written. But I have told you practically nothing of our most important secret, the mystery which inhabits the poet and from which he can never completely separate himself in order to judge it from the outside. I hope it has found a refuge in my poems.

NOTES

1. *Drinking at the Wellspring,* subtitled, *Confidences of Memory and Landscape,* Correa, Paris, 1933 and Gallimard, Paris, 1951. A prose memoir.
2. "Poems of a Melancholy Humor," a group of six poems collected in *Poèmes,* Eugene Figuière, Paris, 1919 and in *L'Escalier,* (*The Stairway*), Gallimard, Paris, 1956.
3. "the black horses of death."
4. "I'm like the one who having hurried too much
   Waits on the road for the carriage to come."
5. Irregular verse.

Reading Poetry
in Public
1951

It's not a simple game of vanity for a poet to recite his poetry in public. Projecting it in this formidable test, he doesn't mind learning whether his work is really finished and transmittable or if some defect will turn against him in the very air.

Indeed, the printed matter that one follows with one's eyes, the silent and unmediated communion between the mute text and the reader, facilitate an unequalled concentration, the more precious because it opens up into an exaltation without witnesses. But isn't poetry made above all for the vocal life? Isn't it waiting for the human voice to release it from the characters of the printing press, from their weight, their silence, their prison, from their apparent indifference?

The human voice, if it is an understanding one, provides poetry with an almost spiritual vehicle. Isn't it the fusion of the body and the mind, a mysterious force that escapes into the air as it reveals itself?

Since there is no deep memory that is not rooted in the heart, the nice gallicisms, *to know by heart, to recite by heart,* are rightful currency in poetry, where Ronsard, Racine, Baudelaire, Hugo, Rimbaud, Valéry, have more than a little to do with the beating of our hearts.

Every day in the lives of men the poetry of the classic poets mingles with the voices of schoolchildren.

> A child stands up in class
> And behold how from the depths of time
> Racine takes his place
> For a moment on his lips.
> Then along comes Jean de la Fontaine
> Who from his fabulous world
> Breathes his poem softly
> To the studious pupil.
> How many falls of snow and rain,
> How many claps of thunder
> Did Villon and Ronsard resist,
> Protected by their poetry!
> How many risings and wars

Did they emerge from alive
As when they were twenty
And recited their poems themselves.

Bergson would like the art of diction not to be considered an art of agreeableness. "Instead of coming at the end of our studies like an ornament, it ought to be at the beginning and throughout, like a support. We would be placing all of our studies on this support if we weren't still yielding to the illusion that the main point is to discourse on things and that you know them sufficiently when you know how to talk about them. But you know and understand only what you can in some measure re-invent."

Whoever recites a poem in public ought to give the impression of creating it in its newborn state. Addressing yourself to an audience is also an effective remedy against the undeserved approval of a poetry that is opaque, untransmittable, and so monotonous that it stifles its own sense as it strains to make it known—an encoded poetry whose code the poet himself doesn't always know, a poetry whose code becomes jumbled the moment he thinks he understands it.

And yet, everything that is forbidden to the poet in life becomes possible and even commendable in transparent poetry . . . the words in his head are enough to present him with palaces, perfumes, women, feasts. Poetry for poets is the art of depriving oneself of nothing and for that very reason to overwhelm the rest of us with everything. Poets happen to consider themselves the Creator and the crowning fact is that they are not entirely wrong, since one re-discovers in their universe all the beasts of the earthly paradise, together with some monsters peculiar to them.

Non-poets forget the fundamental burdens of their various vocations, but the vocation of the poet, Atlas of human suffering, is precisely to remember his burden. In order to lighten it he sings to it and "charms it," as Albert Béguin would say. And even if he writes a stripped-down poetry, it's never so entirely naked that it betrays its distress to us. Poetry, humble as it is, is on the road to opulence. The single star of the Desdichado is dead, but his lute is not the less starry.